From
124 Shor T

Jane Lewis, who has introduced this edition of *Marriage as a Trade* for The Women's Press, has had a long-standing involvement in the feminist movement both in England and in Canada. She is the author of *Politics of Motherhood* (Croom Helm, 1980) and teaches social history and the history of social policy at the London School of Economics.

CICELY HAMILTON

Marriage as a Trade

Introduced by Jane Lewis

The Women's Press

Published by The Women's Press Limited 1981
A member of the Namara Group
124 Shoreditch High Street, London E1 6JE

First published 1909. Copyright under the
Berne Convention.

Introduction copyright © Jane Lewis 1981

Typeset by Dark Moon
Printed in Great Britain by
Redwood Burn Limited, Trowbridge
and bound by Pegasus Bookbinding, Melksham

All rights reserved

British Library Cataloguing in Publication Data

Hamilton, Cicely
  Marriage as a trade.
  1. Marriage
  I. Title
  306.8   HQ728

ISBN 0–7043–3870–X

The Women's Press is a feminist publishing house. We aim to publish books which are lively and original and which reflect the goals of the women's liberation movement.

Our publishing is chiefly in the areas of fiction, literature, politics, health, art history. If you would like to have a complete list of our books please send us an SAE.

The Women's Press also has a book club in which we offer about 50 books a year — our own and other publishers' — at discounts from 25-50% through our quarterly catalogues. Membership costs £5 per year or £10 on a once-only payment basis. Details are also available from us at The Women's Press, 124 Shoreditch High Street, London E1 6JE.

Introduction

Born Cicely Mary Hammill in 1872, Cicely Hamilton changed her name when she left the teaching job she hated to go on the stage. She went on to write plays and novels and also became involved in the early twentieth-century feminist movement which is often associated with the fight for the vote and little else. *Marriage as a Trade* was written at the height of the suffrage struggle but goes behind and beyond it to explore the whole nature of male/female relationships. In particular, it relentlessly strips away the romance surrounding marriage. Hamilton argues that girls are trained to make themselves pleasing to men because marriage is the primary way for women to earn their living. Marriage is thus a trade and the established wisdom is neatly reversed: women are in fact less romantic than men. A man can afford to be romantic in personal relationships, but a woman must play a double game. Love may or may not play a part, but she must 'trap' a man at all costs for her livelihood depends on it. Hamilton's analysis is a personal one. She does not attempt to analyse the structures that give rise to what she describes; the value of her work lies rather in her observations on the relations between men and women and between women, which are extraordinarily perceptive.

Hamilton begins by exploring the romantic image men have of women as 'imperfect and undeveloped creatures' waiting to be made 'perfect and complete' by marriage (pp 20-21). As children, women may also have entertained a romantic picture of love and marriage but little remains of this by the time they reach marriageable age. By then marriage is an economic necessity, the only way of life they have been trained for, yet the desperate desire to succeed in the 'trade' is often accompanied by humiliation. Hamilton illustrates this point in greater detail in her novel, *Just to Get Married* (1911). The heroine, Georgina Vicary, expresses with painful clarity the dilemma of the middle-class, penniless female relative: 'Either I go to a man who is willing and anxious to keep me, or I stay as a burden and a failure with people who are longing to be rid of me. There is no other alternative.'[1] It so happens that a visiting Canadian provides the hope of a man to keep her, and Georgina spends two long weeks trying to entice him into marriage with apparently little success:

> She felt so humbled, so ridiculous, so hateful . . . And if when he went away tomorrow, she would have to keep a high head and a stiff lip before them all [her relatives] whilst they all watched under their eyelids to note her manner of taking it. What a devilish thing it was to be a woman! She wondered if any of them were labouring under the delusion that she was really in love with him. Not likely — at least not likely as far as the women were concerned (p 8).

Georgina's relatives consider it a 'sordid failure' for her not to have got a husband but, as Hamilton's writing shows, the process of *getting* one could also be sordid.

It is also part of Hamilton's argument in *Marriage as a Trade* that women are woefully handicapped in the only trade open to them. In order to remain feminine and appealing, a woman must not appear eager for marriage or 'forward'. No matter that she has been brought up to believe that marriage and motherhood is her destiny, or that she needs economic support; the first move must come from the man. Thus, in *Just to Get Married*, Georgina must use every feminine wile short of actually asking the visiting Canadian to marry her. Hamilton's message is clear: a woman has no bargaining power in choosing the mate who is also her economic lifeline.

Cicely Hamilton also recognises the broader implications of girls' socialisation for marriage. Individuality is squashed out of them. All that is required is the development of enough feminine charm to secure a mate. Hamilton sums up the situation in her characteristically hard-hitting style, the rule becomes: 'Thou shalt not think' (p 46). Men want to believe that a woman is intuitive, if not downright simple-minded. Hamilton quotes a bishop who defined woman as 'a creature who cannot reason and pokes the fire from the top' (p 53). *Marriage as a Trade* argues that women are trained to become what men believe them to be and want them to be, because what men really want is a combination of romance and service: a woman must 'combine the divergent qualities of an inspiration and a good general servant' (p 24).

In short, 'dependence . . . is the essence of wifehood as generally understood by the masculine mind'. As Hamilton saw it, there was but one way out. Women could gain independence only by working for their living. They will be handicapped by lack of proper training and Hamilton also astutely observes that female socialisation will manifest itself in a deferential attitude to men at the workplace:

> Thus a woman will not only decline to call attention to a blunder or oversight on the part of a male fellow-worker, but she will, if possible, cover up his mistake, even suffer by it, and, at any rate will try to give him the impression that it has escaped her notice, and this under circumstances where no sort of injury to the blunderer would be involved, and which would not prevent her from calling prompt attention to a similar slip if made by a colleague of her own sex (p 99).

Cicely Hamilton's observations regarding the difficulties encountered by professional women are as relevant today as they were in 1909. She also noted, and was infuriated by, 'the intrusion of the sexual element into business relations' (p 104), that is, the likelihood that a male employer would hire a pretty girl over a plain one. Hamilton herself had the bitter experience of being thrown out of work twice during her acting career when the company's manager chose to give a role to his mistress.

Hamilton does not attempt to deny that the choice of an independent, self-supporting life is more often than not a hard one. A way out of the marriage trap was offered to Georgina Vicary in *Just to Get Married* by a woman artist who:

> had fought her own battle with the world and it had been a

hard one — at times starvingly hard; but even when she was beaten almost to her knees, for this at least she had learned to thank the gods; that her lot and part was not only to want and watch hungrily for the man in whose eyes she must hope to find favour (p 21).

It is clear where Hamilton's sympathies lie, but Georgina rejects the artist's offer to allow her to share her room because she cannot face the privation that it would entail. Hamilton wrote with feeling as a result of her own experiences. As the daughter of an impoverished army officer, she had also had to find her own way in the world. As an actress she toured with a provincial repertory company for ten years, and later as a writer she shared a single room with her sister. She recorded in her autobiography that life had taught her to expect little and never to count on success.

In her writing she is concerned almost exclusively with the opportunities open to middle-class women although, as her extremely successful play *Diana of Dobson's* showed, her sympathy extended to women working for sweated wages. However, she stuck to her belief that even the hardest of independent working lives was better than the frustration, humiliation and boredom of marriage. The heroine of *Diana of Dobson's*, Diana Massingberd, supports herself as a poorly paid dressmaker throughout her adult life. A small unexpected inheritance enables her to take the holiday of her dreams in Switzerland where she meets a spendthrift guardsman who has never worked for his living, and who imagines her to be the rich widow of *his* dreams. When Diana breaks the news of her real circumstances to him, she pours scorn on his values:

When you thought I had married an old man for his money, you considered that I had acted in a seemly and womanly manner, when you learn that instead of selling myself on the marriage market, I have worked for my living honestly, you consider me impossible.[2]

For Hamilton the issue of independence is very much one of identity, as she said in a debate with G.K. Chesterton in 1911:

'Before your duty to your children, or your duty to your husband comes your duty to yourself.'[3] Hamilton's own independence, her power to 'stand alone', was a source of fierce pride to her and a way of life she would have liked to have seen more women choose.

In all Hamilton's writings there is the assumption that women must choose between marriage (and motherhood) and work. There is no question of the two being successfully combined. This was a common assumption of feminists during the period. Women such as Eleanor Rathbone, who replaced Millicent Garrett Fawcett as President of the major constitutional suffrage society in 1918, leaders of the Women's Labour League, like Ethel Bentham and Mrs J.R. MacDonald, and women trade unionists, like Mary MacArthur, all believed that young children should be cared for at home by their mothers. Charlotte Perkins Gilman, an American, was the only feminist theorist of the period to advocate some form of institutionalised childcare as a means of permitting greater self-development for women with children.[4] This idea was never taken up by the organised British feminist movement, which was more likely to use women's special responsibilities in the home as a strong argument for giving women the vote.

It is clear that Hamilton despaired of any initiative for change coming from married women. By definition, the woman who successfully ensnared a husband was socialised into a helpless and dependent role and developed the 'animal side' of her nature at the expense of the intellectual. Hamilton's impatience with the hopelessness of the position of married women may be compared with Florence Nightingale's earlier outburst entitled 'Cassandra', in which she railed against women who are incapable of sustained thought or conversation, who have nothing to do and who can therefore be interrupted at will and for whom absence from dinner, the great ceremony of the day, is a major calamity.[5] In fact, there may not have been as many late Victorian women of the middle and upper class leading idle lives as has been thought, and the existence of those who did may well not have been so meaningless as has been commonly believed.[6]

Nevertheless, the belief that marriage tended to reduce women to such a state helps to explain the nature of Hamilton's solution to the problem of marriage as a trade. If there was no immediate possibility of a more liberated life within marriage, then the only solution had to be for more women to remain unmarried. These women would prove females to be more than breeding machines and would thus prepare 'a heritage of fuller humanity for the daughters of others' (p 144). Hamilton believed that if it can first be shown that there are reasons for women's existence above and beyond sexual intercourse and reproduction then women's worth would increase and the position of married women be improved indirectly. Future generations of daughters, valued for themselves, would then have a more genuine choice as to whether to marry, because marriage would no longer be the only way of 'earning' a living. It should be noted, though, that they would still have to choose between work and marriage.

Hamilton was extremely anxious to stress that not all women wanted to be wives and mothers and she mocks the idea that married women enjoy more privileges than single women:

I have ascertained the privileges of the married woman to be, at the outside, three in number . . . They are as follows:
1 The right to wear on the third finger of the left hand a gold ring of approved but somewhat monotonous pattern.
2 The right to walk in to dinner in advance of women unfurnished with a gold ring of the approved, monotonous pattern.
3 The right of the wife and mother to peruse openly and in the drawing-room certain forms of literature — such as French novels of an erotic type — which the ordinary unmarried woman is supposed to read only in the seclusion of her bedroom (p 136).

In order to understand why she goes to some length to argue that women can be happy unmarried, it is important to realise how miserable the lot of the unmarried women could be in late Victorian and even Edwardian England. Vera Brittain was of the opinion that 'the cruellest of Victorian institutions was perhaps the old maid'.[7] Hamilton's fictional heroine, Georgina Vicary, captured the essence of the problem when she talked of being unwanted because she was both poor and single. Hamilton herself was very much alive to the inferior status assigned to single women. In her debate in 1911 with G.K. Chesterton she asked bluntly, 'Do you suppose that forty or fifty years ago a woman would have dared to stand up on a platform and say without the slightest shame that she was thirty and unmarried?'[8] Indeed, Hamilton sometimes finds it difficult fully to extend her sympathies to the plight of married women. While Hamilton recognised that married women were encouraged to look down on the unmarried woman, this was something that she nevertheless clearly resented. She commented that while the married woman should be rewarded for careful childrearing, marriage and motherhood per se do not give her the right 'to consider herself my superior' (p 137).

The women's movement in England had begun with the aim of widening employment prospects for single women. In the late 1850s, women such as Barbara Bodichon and Bessie Rayner Parkes set up a Women's Employment Bureau which developed into the Association for the Promotion of the Employment of Women.[9] The Census of 1851, which showed there to be an excess of women in the population, provided the motivation and justification for their efforts. It was no longer possible for all women to get married. Throughout the remainder of the nineteenth century and during the years of the suffrage agitation before World War One, anti-feminists continued to deny any meaningful role for the unmarried woman. The most notable anti-suffrage tract, written by a doctor, Sir Almroth Wright, and published in 1913, explained the militancy of the suffragettes in terms of the 'surplus women' problem. In his view the disturbances could only be stopped by sending the suffragettes to the colonies, where they could successfully be married off.[10] Wright's belief that woman's only possible destiny lay in marriage, and the desperation of a Georgina Vicary to secure a husband, were as much a part of the world we associate with Jane Austen as of the early twentieth century. What makes Georgina Vicary so different from many a nineteenth-century heroine is that she is able to recognise and articulate what marriage actually represents in material terms. Moreover, Hamilton is able in her novels and in *Marriage as a Trade* to offer an alternative to marriage because between the 1860s and 1911 the work opportunities for middle-class women widened significantly; in particular the numbers of clerks and shop assistants had increased dramatically.[11]

In view of their early concern regarding employment, it is not surprising that the Victorian and Edwardian feminist movement in Britain was above all an equal rights movement. It aimed to secure 'a fair field and no favour' and to remove all the disabilities that might hinder women from competing for work on equal terms with men. It followed that women could not ask for special dispensation on account of bearing and rearing children. Again, we are back to the position that women must choose between work and a family. The early feminist movement opposed all protective legislation for women workers, whether it was a matter of restricting the type of occupation open to women and the number of hours of work, or the provision of maternity leave, a position that clearly linked feminists to that brand of laissez-faire individualist who was suspicious of any form of state intervention. Most feminists in the suffrage movement accepted the classical economics doctrines of men such as Henry Fawcett (husband of Millicent Garrett Fawcett, the non-militant suffragist leader), which taught that the adult labour market must be left free to regulate itself.[12] Women trade unionists, conscious of working-class women's need for state regulation of the workplace, were fiercely critical of the feminist position. Mindful above all of the middle-class woman's need for economic independence, and as a self-declared individualist, Hamilton adhered to the traditional feminist claim to a fair field and no favour, even after it had ceased to represent the view of the organised feminist movement. During the interwar period, Hamilton's only public feminist activity consisted of active support for the Open Door Council, an organisation dedicated to securing the freedom for women to work on the same terms as men. She described her reason for supporting the Council in her autobiography:

. . . the Open Door Council had, however, my entire approval, since its aim was to correct the tendency of our legislators to be overkind to women who earn their livelihood; to treat them from youth to age as if they were permanently pregnant, and forbid them all manner of trades and callings in case they might injure their health — forgetting that the first need of women, like the first need of men, is bread to put in their mouths.[13]

At a time when other feminists were trying to analyse the relationship between home and work and were suggesting policies such as family allowances (which in 1918 were put forward as a means of providing independent support for dependents, thus obviating the need for a family wage and making equal pay a possibility), Hamilton remained true to a much older feminist tradition which accepted the separation of the public from the private sphere and believed that work outside the home could not successfully be combined with marriage and motherhood.

Not only did work and family not mix, but Hamilton also made it clear that remaining single also meant remaining celibate. There is no possibility, in Hamilton's writings, of motherhood outside marriage. Ellen Key, a Swedish feminist writing during the same period, believed first that all 'normal' women desired to be mothers, and second that the excess of women over men justified unmarried motherhood.[14] Unlike Key, Hamilton stressed that the 'normal' woman might actually prefer celibacy. The strong defence of celibacy is probably the most puzzling part of *Marriage as a Trade* for the modern reader. It is important not to dismiss it as personal eccentricity on Hamilton's part, although there is undoubtedly an element of this. It is certain that Hamilton experienced an early revulsion to childbearing. In her autobiography she candidly describes two incidents in her early childhood. At the age of three she remembers being horrified by the ugliness of her newborn baby brother and, a little later, her revulsion at the sight of a mother breastfeeding.[15] She has sufficient humour to wonder what the Freudian interpretation of these incidents would be.

More broadly than this, it is important to realise that for Hamilton, as for Charlotte Perkins Gilman, the idea of sexual attraction could not be separated from female socialisation. Both writers refer to the evils of an oversexed womanhood, by which they mean women whose 'feminity' has been developed at the expense of their other (intellectual) attributes and whose roles are thereby confined to the 'animal' ones of sexual partner and nurturer.

Sexuality was not discussed openly in feminist organisations before World War One. It is striking, for instance, that birth control was not publicly debated by feminists until after the war. Hamilton writes of her support for birth control in her autobiography, published in 1935, but does not mention it in *Marriage as a Trade*, although in common with many feminists of the period she called for voluntary motherhood.[16] Abstinence was obviously one way of achieving this.

Feminist writers before World War One all stressed the dangers of motherhood, by which they meant venereal disease. In her book *The Great Scourge and How to End It* (1913), Christabel Pankhurst alleged that between 75 and 80 per cent of all men were infected with gonorrhea. Her solution was to give the vote to women and impose female ideals of chastity on men.[17] For Cicely Hamilton and Charlotte Perkins Gilman, it was all the more outrageous that daughters were kept in ignorance of venereal disease by their mothers because girls had to marry to live. Modern writers have often pointed out that the dangers of venereal disease were much exaggerated by feminists of the period,[18] but the feminist protest must be assessed in the light of three factors. First, the overwhelming resentment at the double moral standard which operated in Victorian England, and which was exemplified by the sexual adventures documented in a volume such as 'Walter's' *My Secret Life*; second, the massive ignorance of married women regarding all aspects of sexuality and childbirth (the Women's Cooperative Guild's collection of *Maternity: Letters from Working Women* showed the misery that resulted from this ignorance)[19] and finally the pressures that were put on women during this period to marry and bear children. The latter came as a result of the falling birth rate, which was felt to threaten Britain's position as an imperial power. As one writer put it: 'In the difference between the number of cradles and the number of coffins lies the existence and persistence of our Empire.'[20] It was during the early years of the twentieth century that the schoolgirl's curriculum was revamped to allow greater time to be devoted to housecraft and motherhood training.[21] Hamilton is referring to these trends when she comments:

> Male humanity has wobbled between two convictions — the one that she [woman] exists for the entire benefit of contemporary manhood; the other, that she exists for the entire benefit of the next generation. The latter is at present the favourite (p 24).

Regardless of whether Hamilton's emphasis on celibacy as the ideal state was either feasible or right, it took great courage at that time to say publicly that not all women wanted children. Most feminists justified the movement towards sexual equality in terms of their traditional roles. For example, Olive Schreiner, who was probably the most influential feminist theorist in England, referred to the deep and overmastering need for motherhood in every virile woman's heart and justified her demand that women be allowed to do whatever work they chose on the grounds that this would strengthen the 'race': parasitic mothers produced 'softened' sons.[22] The vote was also often demanded on the grounds that women as mothers might then be able to secure better protection for their homes, for example by voting for temperance reform.

Hamilton never rejected the basic ideas she expressed in her writing before World War One. As a nurse with the Scottish Women's Hospital Unit during the war she collected more evidence of the male idea that a woman's true destiny is marriage and motherhood. On learning that the whole of the Hospital Unit was staffed by women, a Frenchman commented by way of explanation that they must all have suffered unhappy love affairs. In her autobiography, Hamilton makes a point of saying that she has never regretted her unmarried and childless state, yet it is strange that she does not discuss the writing of *Marriage as a Trade* at all. This is perhaps because she did move towards an explicit rejection of the suffrage movement.

Hamilton was never a militant suffragette but she had, none the less, been active in the movement. In particular, she wrote a suffrage play, *How the Vote was Won*, which was performed at the Royalty Theatre in 1909 (the same year as *Marriage as a Trade* was published) and 'A Pageant of Great Women' for the suffrage exhibition mounted in 1910. After World War One, however, she became preoccupied with finding an explanation for the growth of 'the aggressive instinct' and increasingly came to believe that there was a direct link between the 'lack of control' exhibited by the suffragettes and the larger 'combative impulse' that produced war. As a thorough-going individualist, she above all distrusted 'organised man' and in the suffragette movement, as much as in the fascist youth movements of the 1930s, she saw only people who had resigned their responsible selves to the crowd.

We get a strong sense of the overwhelming effect of the First World War on feminists in the work of Vera Brittain[23] and among feminists generally there was, between 1918 and 1939, a growing preoccupation with world affairs, and in particular the threat posed by fascism. Cicely Hamilton goes further than most though, in her almost disdainful dismissal of the suffrage struggle. This is expressed most clearly in her novel *William an Englishman*, published in 1919. William is an eager socialist prior to World War One and he falls in love with Griselda, 'his exact counterpart in petticoats', a 'blank-minded suburban girl' who is 'enjoying' herself in the suffrage movement. Both are pacifists. Griselda is fond of talking of the peace that will be made by women, while 'exulting in the fighting qualities of her own sex'.[24] William's reading is confined to the *Daily Herald* and Griselda's to the *Suffragette*. They imagine they are fighting a war and speak from 'the profound ignorance of the unread and unimaginative'. They marry in 1914 and it is inevitably the 'real' war that claims both their lives. In an effort to bring to the fore the 'larger issues' — of war and the perils of democracy — Hamilton trivialises and derides the youthful involvement of William and Griselda in the socialist and suffrage movements, which she perceives as thoughtless and narrow, and which she believes to be the direct precursors of larger movements for organised destruction.

Hamilton is a strong and uncompromising writer. One of the male reviewers of *Marriage as a Trade*, writing in a feminist journal, *The Freewoman*, spoke of her 'you be damned' attitude, a quality which he felt marked her as 'the most manlike of women'.[25] The reader today must feel a little wary of her unshaken individualism and self-confessed conservatism, which made her largely unsympathetic to the considerable problems the majority of women would face in pursuing the kind of independent life she advocated. Hamilton was justly proud of her own achievements, but she probably underestimated the difficulties and costs that might be involved for other women forced to choose between love and work. She talks on several occasions of sisterhood, but only with other women who have made it on their own. As Ellen Key pointed out, the choice between family duties, duties to oneself and duties to society is not an easy one to make in practice and it may well be that the early feminist movement underestimated the need women have for love and affection.

Hamilton's insistence that women must be valued for themselves, and not in relation to husband or children, is central to any feminist analysis, but her insistence on equality on male terms, which might well necessitate the rejection of sexuality and children, must be suspect. Again, as Key put it: 'equality of the sexes [does not] imply sameness of the sexes'.[26] Questions concerning the nature of equality and the balance that can be achieved between work and family life are far from settled issues in the women's liberation movement today and Hamilton's views should at least provoke fresh thought. It is, after all, remarkable that since she wrote *Marriage as a Trade* not only have married women entered the labour force in unparalleled numbers, but also the average age of women at marriage has shown a steady decline and the romantic image of the white wedding shows little sign of diminishing attraction.

Notes

1. Cicely Hamilton, *Just to get Married* (London, Chapman Hall, 1911), p 89.
2. Cicely Hamilton, *Diana of Dobson's* (New York, Century Co, 1908), pp 265-6.
3. Report of the debate in *The Vote* 3, 15 April 1911, p 295.
4. C.P. Gilman, *Women and Economics* (New York, Harper Torchbooks, 1966), 1st ed. 1898; *The Man Made World* (London, T. Fisher Unwin, 1911); and *Concerning Children*

London, Watts and Co, 1907).

5   Florence Nightingale, 'Cassandra', in Ray Strachey, *The Cause* (London, Virago, 1979), 1st ed. 1928, pp 395-418.
6   See Patricia Branca, *Silent Sisterhood* (London, Croom Helm, 1975), and Leonore Davidoff, *The Best Circles* (London, Croom Helm, 1973).
7   Vera Brittain, *Lady into Woman* (Andrew Dakers, 1953), p 233.
8   *The Vote* 3, 15 April 1911, p 295.
9   For an account of this, see Strachey, *The Cause*.
10 Sir Almroth E. Wright, *The Unexpurgated Case Against Woman Suffrage* (London, Constable, 1913).
11 Lee Holcombe, *Victorian Ladies at Work* (Newton Abbott, David and Charles, 1973).
12 Many of the views of the organised feminist movement's leadership were as extreme as those of the philosopher, Herbert Spencer, who abhorred all and any action by the state. Rodney Barker gives the context for their views in *Political Ideas in Modern Britain* (London, Methuen, 1978).
13 Hamilton, *Life Errant* (London, J.M. Dent, 1935) pp 288-9.
14 Ellen Key, *The Woman Movement* (London, G.P. Putnams, 1912.
15 Hamilton, *Life Errant*, p 5.
16 For an analysis of the concept of 'voluntary motherhood', see Angus McLaren, *Birth Control in Nineteenth-Century England* (London, Croom Helm, 1978), and Linda Gordon, *Woman's Body Woman's Right* (New York, Grossman, 1976).
17 Christabel Pankhurst, *The Great Scourge and How to End It* (London, E. Pankhurst, 1913).
18 See, for example, Andrew Rosen's analysis of the militant suffragette movement, *Rise Up Women* (London, Routledge, 1974), pp 208-10.
19 M. Llewellyn Davies (ed), *Maternity: Letters from Working Women* (London, Virago, 1978), 1st ed. 1915.
20 J. Marchant, *Cradles or Coffins* (London, by the author, 1916).
21 See Carol Dyhouse, 'Social Darwinistic Ideas and Women's Education', *History of Education* 5 (1976), and Anna

David 'Imperialism and Motherhood', *History Workshop Journal* 5 (1978).
22   Olive Schreiner, *Woman and Labour* (London, Virago, 1978), 1st ed. 1911, p 79 et. seq.
23   Vera Brittain, *Testament of Youth* (London, Virago, 1978), 1st ed. 1933.
24   Cicely Hamilton, *William an Englishman* (London, Skeffington, 1919), p 21.
25   William Foss in *The Freewoman* 1, 18 April 1912.
26   Key, *The Woman Movement*, p 181.

A Note on Cicely Hamilton's Work

Cicely Hamilton (1872-1952) had an active writing career that spanned two world wars. Novels and plays not mentioned in the text above include *A Matter of Money* (1916), *Senlis* (1917), *Theodore Savage* (1922), *The Old Adam* (1926), *Full Stop* (1931), *The Beggar Prince* (1944), and two plays for children: *The Child in Flanders* (1922), and *Mr. Pompous and the Pussy Cat* (1948).

Hamilton also wrote a large number of travel books during the 1930s, a history of the Old Vic with Lilian Baylis (1926) and, in keeping with her preoccupation with aggression during the 1930s, *Lament for Democracy* (1940).

Preface

The only excuse for this book is the lack of books on the subject with which it deals — the trade aspect of marriage. That is to say, wifehood and motherhood considered as a means of livelihood for women.

I shall not deny for an instant that there are aspects of matrimony other than the trade aspect; but upon these there is no lack of a very plentiful literature — the love of man and woman has been written about since humanity acquired the art of writing.

The love of man and woman is, no doubt, a thing of infinite importance; but also of infinite importance is the manner in which woman earns her bread and the economic conditions under which she enters the family and propagates the race. Thus an inquiry into the circumstances under which the wife and mother plies her trade seems to me quite as necessary and justifiable as an inquiry into the conditions of other and less important industries — such as mining or cotton-spinning. It will not be disputed that the manner in which a human being earns his livelihood tends to mould and influence his character — to warp or to improve it. The man who works amidst brutalising surroundings is apt to become brutal; the man from whom intelligence is demanded is apt to exercise it. Particular trades tend to develop particular types; the boy who becomes a soldier will not turn out in all respects the man he would have been had he decided to enter a stockbroker's office. In the same way the trade of marriage tends to produce its own particular type; and my contention is that woman, as we know her, is largely the product of the conditions imposed upon her by her staple industry.

I am not of those who are entirely satisfied with woman as she is; on the contrary, I consider that we are greatly in need of improvement, mental, physical and moral. And it is because I desire such improvement — not only in our own interests but in that of the race in general — that I desire to see an alteration in the conditions of our staple industry. I have no intention of attacking the institution of marriage in itself — the life companionship of man and woman; I merely wish to point out that there are certain grave disadvantages attaching to that institution as it exists to-day. These disadvantages I believe to be largely unnecessary and avoidable; but at present they are very real, and the results produced by them are anything but favourable to the mental, physical and moral development of woman.

One

The sense of curiosity is, as a rule, aroused in us only by the unfamiliar and the unexpected. What custom and long usage has made familiar we do not trouble to inquire into but accept without comment or investigation; confusing the actual with the inevitable, and deciding, slothfully enough, that the thing that is is, likewise, the thing that was and is to be. In nothing is this inert and slothful attitude of mind more marked than in the common, unquestioning acceptance of the illogical and unsatisfactory position occupied by women. And it is the prevalence of that attitude of mind which is the only justification for a book which purports to be nothing more than the attempt of an unscientific woman to explain, honestly and as far as her limitations permit, the why and wherefore of some of the disadvantages under which she and her sisters exist — the reason why their place in the world into which they were born is often so desperately and unnecessarily uncomfortable.

I had better, at the outset, define the word 'woman' as I understand and use it, since it is apt to convey two distinct and differing impressions, according to the sex of the hearer. My conception of woman is inevitably the feminine conception; a thing so entirely unlike the masculine conception of woman that it is eminently needful to define the term and make my meaning clear; lest, when I speak of woman in my own tongue, my reader, being male, translate the expression, with confusion as the result.

By a woman, then, I understand an individual human being whose life is her own concern; whose worth, in my eyes (worth being an entirely personal matter) is in no way advanced or detracted from by the accident of marriage; who does not rise in my estimation by reason of a purely physical capacity for bearing children, or sink in my estimation through a lack of that capacity. I am quite aware, of course, that her life, in many cases, will have been moulded to a great extent by the responsibilities of marriage and the care of children; just as I am aware that the lives of most of the men with whom I am acquainted have been moulded to a great extent by the trade or profession by which they earn their bread. But my judgment of her and appreciation of her are a personal judgment and appreciation, having nothing to do with her actual or potential relations, sexual or maternal, with other people. In short, I never think of her either as a wife or as a mother — I separate the woman from her attributes. To me she is an entity in herself; and if, on meeting her for the first time, I inquire whether or no she is married, it is only because I wish to know whether I am to address her as Mrs or Miss.

That, frankly and as nearly as I can define it, is my attitude towards my own sex; an attitude which, it is almost needless to say, I should not insist upon if I did not believe that it was fairly typical and that the majority of women, if they analysed their feelings on the subject, would find that they regarded each other in much the same way.

It is hardly necessary to point out that the mental attitude of the average man towards woman is something quite different from this. It is a mental attitude reminding one of that of the bewildered person who could not see the wood for the trees. To him the accidental factor in woman's life is the all-important and his conception of her has never got beyond her attributes — and certain only of these. As far as I can make out, he looks upon her as something having a definite and necessary physical relation to man; without that definite and necessary relation she is, as the cant phrase goes, 'incomplete'. That is to say, she is not woman at all — until man has made her so. Until the moment when he takes her in hand she is merely the raw material of womanhood — the undeveloped and unfinished article.

Without sharing in the smallest degree this estimate of her own destiny, any fair-minded woman must admit its advantages from the point of view of the male — must sympathise with the pleasurable sense of importance, creative power, even of artistry, which such a conviction must impart. To take the imperfect and undeveloped creature and, with a kiss upon her lips and a ring upon her finger, to make of her a woman, perfect and complete — surely a prerogative almost divine in its magnificence, most admirable, most enviable!

It is this consciousness, expressed or unexpressed, (frequently the former) of his own supreme importance in her destiny that colours every thought and action of man towards woman. Having assumed that she is incomplete without him, he draws the quite permissible conclusion that she exists only for the purpose of attaining to completeness through him — and that where she does not so attain to it, the unfortunate creature is, for all practical purposes, non-existent. To him womanhood is summed up in one of its attributes — wifehood, or its unlegalised equivalent. Language bears the stamp of the idea that woman is a wife, actually, or in embryo. To most men — perhaps to all — the girl is some man's wife that is to be; the married woman some man's wife that is; the widow some man's wife that was; the spinster some man's wife that should have been — a damaged article, unfit for use, unsuitable. Therefore a negligible quantity.

I have convinced myself, by personal observation and inquiry, that my description of the male attitude in this respect is in no way exaggerated. It has, for instance, fallen to my lot, over and over again, to discuss with men — most of them distinctly above the average in intelligence — questions affecting the welfare and conditions of women. And over and over again, after listening to their views for five minutes or so, I have broken in upon them and pulled them up with the remark that they were narrowing down the subject under discussion — that what they were considering was not the claim of women in general, but the claim of a particular class — the class of wives and mothers. I may add that the remark has invariably been received with an expression of extreme astonishment. And is it not on record that Henley once dashed across a manuscript the terse pronouncement, 'I take no interest in childless women'? Comprehensive; and indicating a confusion in the author's mind between the terms woman and breeding-machine. Did it occur to him, I wonder, that the poor objects of his scorn might venture to take some interest in themselves? Probably he did not credit them with so much presumption.

The above has, I hope, explained in how far my idea of woman differs from male ideas on the same subject and has also made it clear that I do not look upon women as persons whose destiny it is to be married. On the contrary, I hold, and hold very strongly, that the narrowing down of woman's hopes and ambitions to the sole pursuit and sphere of marriage is one of the principal causes of the various disabilities, economic and otherwise, under which she labours today. And I hold, also, that this concentration of all her hopes and ambitions on the one object was, to a great extent, the result of artificial pressure, of unsound economic and social conditions — conditions which forced her energy into one channel, by the simple expedient of depriving it of every other outlet, and made marriage practically compulsory.

To say the least of it, marriage is no more essentially necessary to woman than to man — one would imagine that it was rather the other way about. There are a good many drawbacks attached to the fulfilment of a woman's destiny; in an unfettered state of existence it is possible that they might weigh more heavily with her than they can do at present — being balanced, and more than balanced, by artificial means. I am inclined to think that they would. The institution of marriage by capture, for instance, has puzzled many inquirers into the habits of primitive man. It is often, I believe, regarded as symbolic; but why should it not point to a real reluctance to be reduced to permanent servitude on the part of primitive woman — a reluctance comprehensible enough, since, primitive woman's wants being few and easily supplied by herself, there was no need for her to exchange possession of her person for the means of existence?

It is Nietzsche, if I remember rightly, who has delivered himself of the momentous opinion that everything in woman is a riddle, and that the answer to the riddle is child-bearing. Child-bearing certainly explains some qualities in woman — for instance her comparative fastidiousness in sexual relations — but not all. If it did, there would be no riddle — yet Nietzsche admits that one exists. Nor is he alone in his estimate of the 'mysterious' nature of woman; her unfathomable and erratic character, her peculiar aptitude for appearing 'uncertain, coy, and hard to please', has been insisted upon time after time — insisted upon alike as a charm and a deficiency. A charm because of its unexpected, a deficiency because of its unreasonable, quality.

Woman, in short, is not only a wife and mother, but a thoroughly incomprehensible wife and mother.

Now it seems to me that a very simple explanation of this mystery which perpetually envelops our conduct and impulses can be found in the fact that the fundamental natural laws which govern them have never been ascertained or honestly sought for. Or rather — since the fundamental natural laws which govern us are the same large and simple laws which govern other animals, man included — though they have been ascertained, the masculine intellect has steadfastly and stubbornly refused to admit that they can possibly apply to us in the same degree as to every other living being. As a substitute for these laws, he suggests explanations of his own — for the most part flattering to himself. He believes, apparently, that we live in a world apart, governed by curious customs and regulations of our own — customs and regulations which 'have no fellow in the universe.' Once the first principle of natural law was recognised as applying to us, we should cease to be so unfathomable, erratic, and unexpected to the wiseacres and poets who spend their time in judging us by rule of thumb, and expressing amazement at the unaccountable and contradictory results.

I do not know whether it is essentially impossible for man to approach us in the scientific spirit, but it has not yet been done. (To approach motherhood or marriage in the scientific spirit is, of course, not in the least the same thing.) His attitude towards us has been by turns — and sometimes all at once — adoring, contemptuous, sentimental, and savage — anything, in short, but open-minded and deductive. The result being that different classes, generations, and peoples have worked out their separate and impressionistic estimates of woman's meaning in the scheme of things — the said estimates frequently clashing with those of other classes, generations, and peoples. The Mahometan, for instance, after careful observation from his point of view, decided that she was flesh without a soul, and to be treated accordingly; the troubadour seems to have found in her a spiritual incentive to aspiration in deed and song. The early Fathers of the Church, who were in the habit of giving troubled and nervous consideration to the subject, denounced her, at spasmodic intervals, as sin personified. What the modern man understands by woman I have already explained; and he further expects his theory to materialise and embody itself in a being who combines the divergent qualities of an inspiration and a good general servant. He is often disappointed.

All these are rule of thumb definitions, based on insufficient knowledge and inquiry, which, each in its turn, has been accepted, acted upon, and found wanting. Each of the generations and classes mentioned — and many more beside — has worked out its own theory of woman's orbit (round man); and has subsequently found itself in the position of the painstaking astronomer who, after having mapped the pathway of a newly-discovered heavenly body to his own satisfaction, suddenly finds his calculations upset, and the heavenly body swerving off through space towards some hitherto unexpected centre of attraction. The theory of the early Fathers was upset before it was enunciated — for sin personified had wept at the foot of the Cross, and men adored her for it. The modern angel with the cookery-book under her wing has expressed an open and pronounced dislike to domestic service, and cheerfully discards her wings to fight her way into the liberal professions. And those who hold fast to the Nietzschean theory that motherhood is the secret and justification of woman's existence, must be somewhat bewildered by latter-day episcopal lamentations over the unwillingness of woman to undergo the pains and penalties of childbirth, and by the reported intention of an American State Legislature to stimulate a declining birthrate by the payment of one dollar for each child born. One feels that the strength of an instinct that has, in an appreciable number of cases, to be stimulated by the offer of four shillings and twopence must have been somewhat overestimated. No wonder woman is a mystery in her unreliability; she has broken every law of her existence, and does so day by day.

As a matter of fact, the various explanations which have been given for woman's existence can be narrowed down to two — her husband and her child. Male humanity has wobbled between two convictions — the one, that she exists for the entire benefit of contemporary mankind; the other, that she exists for the entire benefit of the next generation. The latter is at present the favourite. One consideration only male humanity has firmly refused to entertain — that she exists in any degree whatsoever for the benefit of herself. In consequence, woman is the one animal from whom he demands that it shall deviate from, and act in defiance of, the first law of nature — self-preservation.

It seems baldly ridiculous, of course, to state in so many words that that first and iron law applies to women as well as to men, birds, and beetles. No one in cold blood or cold ink would contradict the obvious statement; but all the same, I maintain that I am perfectly justified in asserting that the average man does mentally and unconsciously except the mass of women from the workings of that universal law.

To give a simple and familiar instance. Year by year there crops up in the daily newspapers a grumbling and sometimes acrid correspondence on the subject of the incursion of women into a paid labour market formerly monopolised by their brothers. (The unpaid labour market, of course, has always been open to them.) The tone taken by the objector is instructive and always the same. It is pointed out to us that we are working for less than a fair wage; that we are taking the bread out of the mouths of men; that we are filching the earnings of a possible husband and thereby lessening, or totally destroying, our chances of matrimony.

The first objection is, of course, legitimate, and is shared by the women to whom it applies; from the others one can only infer that it is an impertinence in a woman to be hungry, and that, in the opinion of a large number of persons who write to the newspapers, the human female is a creature capable of living on air and the hopes of a possible husband. The principle that it is impolite to mention a certain organ of the body which requires to be replenished two or three times a day is, in the case of a woman, carried so far that it is considered impolite of her even to possess that organ; and as a substitute for the wages wherewith she buys food to fill it, she is offered the lifting of a hat and the resignation of a seat in a tramcar. She rejects the offer, obeys the first law of nature, and is rebuked for it — the human male, bred in the conviction that she lives for him alone, standing aghast. Some day he will discover that woman does not support life only in order to obtain a husband, but frequently obtains a husband only in order to support life.

The above is, to my mind, a clear and familiar instance of the manner in which man is accustomed to take for granted our exemption from a law from which there is no exemption. It matters not whether or no he believes, in so many words, that we need not eat in order that we may not die; the point is, that he acts as if he believed it. (The extreme reluctance of local authorities to spend any of the money at their disposal on unemployed women is a case in point. It would be ridiculous to ascribe it to animosity towards the women themselves — it must arise, therefore, from a conviction that the need of the foodless woman is not so pressing as the need of the foodless man.) And it is because I have so often come in contact with the state of mind that makes such delusions possible, that I have thought it necessary to insist on the fact that self-preservation is the first law of our being. The purpose of race-preservation, which is commonly supposed to be the excuse for our existence, is, and must be, secondary and derivative; it is quite impossible for a woman to bring children into the world unless she has first obtained the means of supporting her own life. How to eat, how to maintain existence, is the problem that has confronted woman, as well as man, since the ages dawned for her. Other needs and desires may come later; but the first call of life is for the means of supporting it.

To support life it is necessary to have access to the fruits of the earth, either directly — as in the case of the agriculturist — or indirectly, and through a process of exchange as the price of work done in other directions. And in this process of exchange woman, as compared with her male fellow-worker, has always been at a disadvantage. The latter, even where direct access to the earth was denied to him, has usually been granted some measure of choice as to the manner in which he would pay for the necessities the earth produced for him — that is to say, he was permitted to select the trade by which he earned his livelihood. From woman, who has always been far more completely excluded from direct access to the necessities of life, who has often been barred, both by law and by custom, from the possession of property, one form of payment was demanded, and one only. It was demanded of her that she should enkindle and satisfy the desire of the male, who would thereupon admit her to such share of the property he possessed or earned as should seem good to him. In other words, she exchanged, by the ordinary process of barter, possession of her person for the means of existence.

Whether such a state of things is natural or unnatural I do not pretend to say; but it is, I understand, peculiar to women, having no exact counterpart amongst the females of other species. Its existence, at any rate, justifies us in regarding marriage as essentially (from the woman's point of view) a commercial or trade undertaking. By marriage she earned her bread; and as the instinct of self-preservation drove man forth to hunt, to till the soil, to dig beneath it — to cultivate his muscles and his brain so that he might get the better of nature and his rivals — so brute necessity and the instinct of self-preservation in woman urged and enjoined on her the cultivation of those narrow and particular qualities of mind and body whereby desire might be excited and her wage obtained.

A man who was also a poet has thoughtfully explained that:

'Man's love is of man's life a thing apart,
'Tis woman's whole existence.'

(It must be very pleasant to be a man and to entertain that conviction.) Translated into feminine and vulgar prose, the effusion runs something like this:

The housekeeping trade is the only one open to us — so we enter the housekeeping trade in order to live. This is not always quite the same as entering the housekeeping trade in order to love.

No one can imagine that it is the same who has ever heard one haggard, underpaid girl cry to another, in a burst of bitter confidence:

'I would marry any one, to get out of this.'

Which, if one comes to think of it, is hard on 'any one'.

Two

If I am right in my view that marriage for woman has always been not only a trade, but a trade that is practically compulsory, I have at the same time furnished an explanation of the reason why women, as a rule, are so much less romantic than men where sexual attraction is concerned. Where the man can be single-hearted, the woman necessarily is double-motived. It is, of course, the element of commerce and compulsion that accounts for this difference of attitude; an impulse that may have to be discouraged, nurtured or simulated to order — that is, at any rate, expected, for commercial or social reasons to put in an appearance as a matter of course and at the right and proper moment — can never have the same vigour, energy and beauty as an impulse that is unfettered and unforced.

More than once in my life I have been struck by the beauty of a man's honest conception and ideal of love and marriage — a conception and ideal which one comes across in unexpected and unlikely persons and which is by no means confined to those whose years are still few in number and whose hearts are still hot within them. Only a few weeks ago I heard an elderly gentleman of scientific attainments talk something which, but for its sincerity, would have seemed to me sheer sentimental balderdash concerning the relations of men and women. And from other equally respectable gentlemen I have heard opinions that were beautiful as well as honest on the relations of the sexes, of a kind that no woman, being alone with another woman, would ever venture to utter. For we see the thing differently. I am not so foolish as to imagine that theory and practice in this or any other matter are in the habit of walking hand in hand; I know that for men the word love has two different meanings and therefore I should be sorry to have to affirm on oath that the various gentlemen who have, at various times, favoured me with their views on the marriage question have one and all lived up to their convictions; but at least their conception of the love and duty owed by man and woman to each other was a high one, honourable, not wanting in reverence, not wanting in romance. Over and over again I have heard women unreticent enough upon the same subject; but, when they spoke their hearts, the picturesque touch — the flash and fire of romance — was never nearly so strong and sometimes altogether absent.

And I have never seen love — the sheer passionate and personal delight in and worship of a being of the other sex — so vividly and uncontrollably expressed on the face of a woman as on the face of a man. I have with me, as one of the things not to be forgotten, the memory of a cheap foreign hotel where, two or three years back, a little Cockney clerk was making holiday in worshipful attendance on the girl he was engaged to. At table I used to watch him, being very sure that he had no eyes for me; and once or twice I had the impulse that I should like to speak to him and thank him for what he had shown me. I have seen women in love time after time, but none in whom the fire burned as it burned in him — consumedly. I used to hope his Cockney goddess would have understanding at least to reverence the holy thing that passed the love of women . . . .

How should it be otherwise — this difference in the attitude of man and woman in their relations to each other? To make them see and feel more alike in the matter, the conditions under which they live and bargain must be made more alike. With even the average man love and marriage may be something of a high adventure, entered upon whole-heartedly and because he so desires. With the average woman it is not a high adventure — except in so far as adventure means risk — but a destiny or necessity. If not a monetary necessity, then a social. (How many children, I wonder, are born each year merely because their mothers were afraid of being called old maids? One can imagine no more inadequate reason for bringing a human being into the world.) The fact that her destiny, when he arrives, may be all that her heart desires and deserves does not prevent him from being the thing that, from her earliest years, she had, for quite other reasons, regarded as inevitable. Quite consciously and from childhood the 'not impossible he' is looked upon, not simply as an end desirable in himself, but as a means of subsistence. The marriageable man may seek his elective affinity until he find her; the task of the marriageable woman is infinitely more complicated, since her elective affinity has usually to be combined with her bread and butter. The two do not always grow in the same place.

What is the real, natural and unbiassed attitude of woman towards love and marriage it is perfectly impossible for even a woman to guess at under present conditions, and it will continue to be impossible for just so long as the natural instincts of her sex are inextricably interwoven with, thwarted and deflected by, commercial considerations. When — if ever — the day of woman's complete social and economic independence dawns upon her, when she finds herself free and upright in a new world where no artificial pressure is brought to bear upon her natural inclinations or disinclinations, then, and then only, will it be possible to untwist a tangled skein and judge to what extent and what precise degree she is swayed by those impulses, sexual and maternal, which are now, to the exclusion of every other factor, presumed to dominate her existence. And not only to dominate, but to justify it. (A presumption, by the way, which seems to ignore the fact — incompatible, surely, with the theory of 'incompleteness' — that celibacy irks the woman less than it does the man.)

What, one wonders, would be the immediate result if the day of independence and freedom from old restrictions were to dawn suddenly and at once? Would it be to produce, at first and for a time, a rapid growth amongst all classes of women of that indifference to, and almost scorn of, marriage which is so marked a characteristic of the — alas, small — class who can support themselves in comfort by work which is congenial to them? Perhaps — for a time, until the revulsion was over and things righted themselves. (I realise, of course, that it is quite impossible for a male reader to accept the assertion that any one woman, much less any class of women, however small its numbers, can be indifferent to or scornful of marriage — which would be tantamount to admitting that she could be indifferent to or scornful of himself. What follows, therefore, can only appear to him as an ineffectual attempt on the part of an embittered spinster to explain that the grapes are sour; and he is courteously requested to skip to the end of the chapter. It would be lost labour on my part to seek to disturb his deep-rooted conviction that all women who earn decent incomes in intelligent and interesting ways are too facially unpleasant to be placed at the head of a dinner-table. I shall not attempt to disturb that conviction; I make it a rule never to attempt the impossible.) This new-born attitude of open indifference and contempt, while perhaps appearing strained and unnatural, is, it seems to me, a natural one enough for women whose daily lives have falsified every tradition in which they were born and bred.

For the tradition handed down from generations to those girl children who now are women grown was, with exceptions few and far between, the one tradition of marriage — marriage as inevitable as lessons and far more inevitable than death. Ordering dinner and keeping house: that we knew well, and from our babyhood was all the future had to give to us. For the boys there would be other things; wherefore our small hearts bore a secret grudge against Almighty God that He had not made us boys — since their long thoughts were our long thoughts, and together we wallowed in cannibals and waxed clamorous over engines. For them, being boys, there might be cannibals and engines in the world beyond; but for us — oh, the flat sameness of it! — was nothing but a husband, ordering dinner and keeping house. Therefore we dreamed of a settler for a husband, and of assisting him to shoot savages with a double-barrelled gun. So might the round of household duties be varied and most pleasantly enlivened.

Perhaps it was the stolid companionship of the doll, perhaps the constant repetition of the formula 'when you have children of your own' that precluded any idea of shirking the husband and tackling the savage off our own bat. For I cannot remember that we ever shirked him. We selected his profession with an eye to our own interests; he was at various times a missionary, a sailor and a circus-rider; but from the first we recognised that he was unavoidable. We planned our lives and knew that he was lurking vaguely in the background to upset our best-laid calculations. We were still very young, I think, when we realised that his shadowy personality was an actual, active factor in our lives; that it was because of him and his surmised desires that our turbulent inclinations were thwarted and compressed into narrow channels, and that we were tamed and curbed as the boys were never tamed and curbed. When that which the boys might do with impunity was forbidden to us as a sin of the first water, we knew that it was because he would not like it. The thought was not so consciously expressed, perhaps; but it was there and lived with us. So we grew up under his influence, presuming his wishes, and we learned, because of him, to say, 'I can't,' where our brothers said, 'I can,' and to believe, as we had been taught, that all things, save a very few (such as ordering dinner and keeping house) were not for us because we were not men. (Yet we had our long, long thoughts — we had them, too!) That was one thing that he desired we should believe; and another was that only through him could we attain to satisfaction and achievement; that our every desire that was not centred upon him and upon his children would be barren and bitter as dead-sea ashes in the mouth. We believed that for a long time . . . .

And he was certain to come: the only question was, when? When he came we should fall in love with him, of course — and he would kiss us — and there would be a wedding . . . .

Some of us — and those not a few — started life equipped for it after this fashion; creatures of circumstance who waited to be fallen in love with. That was indeed all; we stood and waited — on approval. And then came life itself and rent our mother's theories to tatters. For we discovered — those of us, that is, who were driven out to work that we might eat — we discovered very swiftly that what we had been told was the impossible was the thing we had to do. That and no other. So we accomplished it, in fear and trembling, only because we had to; and with that first achievement of the impossible the horizon widened with a rush, and the implanted, hampering faith in our own poor parasitic uselessness began to wither at the root and die. We had learned to say, 'I can.' And as we went on, at first with fear and then with joy, from impossibility to impossibility, we looked upon the world with new eyes.

To no man, I think, can the world be quite as wonderful as it is to the woman now alive who has fought free. Those who come after her will enter by right of birth upon what she attains by right of conquest; therefore, neither to them will it be the same. The things that to her brother are common and handed down, to her are new possessions, treasured because she herself has won them and no other for her. It may well be that she attaches undue importance to these; it could scarcely be otherwise. Her traditions have fallen away from her, her standard of values is gone. The old gods have passed away from her, and as yet the new gods have spoken with no very certain voice. The world to her is in the experimental stage. She grew to womanhood weighed down by the conviction that life held only one thing for her; and she stretches out her hands to find that it holds many. She grew to womanhood weighed down by the conviction that her place in the scheme of things was the place of a parasite; and she knows (for necessity has taught her) that she has feet which need no support. She is young in the enjoyment of her new powers and has a pleasure that is childish in the use of them. By force of circumstances her faith has been wrested from her and the articles of her new creed have yet to be tested by experience — her own. Her sphere — whatever it may prove to be — no one but herself can define for her. Authority to her is a broken reed. Has she not heard and read solemn disquisitions by men of science on the essential limitations of woman's nature and the consequent impossibility of activity in this or that direction? — knowing, all the while, that what they swear to her she cannot do she does, is doing day by day!

Some day, no doubt, the pendulum will adjust itself and swing true; a generation brought up to a wider horizon as a matter of course will look around it with undazzled eyes and set to work to reconstruct the fundamental from the ruins of what was once esteemed so. But in the mean time the new is — new; the independence that was to be as dead-sea ashes in our mouth tastes very sweet indeed; and the unsheltered life that we were taught to shrink from means the fighting of a good fight . . . .

Selfishness, perhaps — all selfishness — this pleasure in ourselves and in the late growth of that which our training had denied us. But then, from our point of view, the sin and crime of woman in the past has been a selflessness which was ignoble because involuntary. Our creed may be vague as yet, but one article thereof is fixed: there is no merit in a sacrifice which is compulsory, no virtue in a gift which is not a gift but a tribute.

Three

I have insisted so strongly upon what I believe to be the attitude towards life of the independent woman mainly with the object of proving my assertion that there are other faculties in our nature besides those which have hitherto been forced under a hothouse system of cultivation — sex and motherhood. It is quite possible that a woman thinking, feeling and living in a manner I have described may be dubbed unsexed; but even if she be what is technically termed unsexed, it does not follow therefore that she is either unnatural or unwomanly. Sex is only one of the ingredients of the natural woman — an ingredient which has assumed undue and exaggerated proportions in her life owing to the fact that it has for many generations furnished her with the means of livelihood.

In sexual matters it would appear that the whole trend and tendency of man's relations to woman has been to make refusal impossible and to cut off every avenue of escape from the gratification of his desire. His motive in concentrating all her energy upon the trade of marriage was to deny it any other outlet. The original motive was doubtless strengthened, as time went on, by an objection to allowing her to come into economic competition with him; but this was probably a secondary or derivative cause of his persistent refusal to allow her new spheres of activity, having its primary root in the consciousness that economic independence would bring with it the power of refusal.

The uncompromising and rather brutal attitude which man has consistently adopted towards the spinster is, to my mind, a confirmation of this theory. (The corresponding attitude of the married woman towards her unmarried sister I take to be merely servile and imitative.) It was not only that the creature was chaste and therefore inhuman. That would have justified neglect and contempt on his part, but not the active dislike he always appears to have entertained for her. That active and somewhat savage dislike must have had its origin in the consciousness that the perpetual virgin was a witness, however reluctantly, to the unpalatable fact that sexual intercourse was not for every woman an absolute necessity; and this uneasy consciousness on his part accounts for the systematic manner in which he placed the spinster outside the pale of a chivalry, upon which, from her unprotected position, one would have expected her to have an especial claim.

If it be granted that marriage is, as I have called it, essentially a trade on the part of woman — the exchange of her person for the means of subsistence — it is legitimate to inquire into the manner in which that trade is carried on, and to compare the position of the worker in the matrimonial with the position of the worker in any other market. Which brings us at once to the fact — arising from the compulsory nature of the profession — that it is carried on under disadvantages unknown and unfelt by those who earn their living by other methods. For the regulations governing compulsory service — the institution of slavery and the like — are always framed, not in the interests of the worker, but in the interests of those who impose his work upon him. The regulations governing exchange and barter in the marriage market, therefore, are necessarily framed in the interests of the employer — the male.

The position is this. Marriage, with its accompaniments and consequences — the ordering of a man's house, the bearing and rearing of his children — has, by the long consent of ages, been established as practically the only means whereby woman, with honesty and honour, shall earn her daily bread. Her every attempt to enter any other profession has been greeted at first with scorn and opposition; her sole outlook was to be dependence upon man. Yet the one trade to which she is destined, the one means of earning her bread to which she is confined, she may not openly profess. No other worker stands on the same footing. The man who has his bread to earn, with hands, or brains, or tools, goes out to seek for the work to which he is trained; his livelihood depending on it, he offers his skill and services without shame or thought of reproach. But with woman it is not so; she is expected to express unwillingness for the very work for which she has been taught and trained. She has been brought up in the belief that her profession is marriage and motherhood; yet though poverty may be pressing upon her — though she may be faced with actual lack of the necessities of life — she must not openly express her desire to enter that profession, and earn her bread in the only way for which she is fitted. She must stand aside and wait — indefinitely; and attain to her destined livelihood by appearing to despise it.

That, of course, is the outcome of something more than a convention imposed on her by man; nature, from the beginning, has made her more fastidious and reluctant than the male. But with this natural fastidiousness and reluctance the commercialism imposed upon her by her economic needs is constantly at clash and at conflict, urging her to get her bread as best she can in the only market open to her. Theoretically — since by her wares she lives — she has a perfect right to cry those wares and seek to push them to the best advantage. That is to say, she has a perfect right to seek, with frankness and with openness, the man who, in her judgment, can most fittingly provide her with the means of support.

This freedom of bargaining to the best advantage, permitted as a matter of course to every other worker, is denied to her. It is, of course, claimed and exercised by the prostitute class — a class which has pushed to its logical conclusion the principle that woman exists by virtue of a wage paid her in return for the possession of her person; but it is interesting to note that the 'unfortunate' enters the open market with the hand of the law extended threateningly above her head. The fact is curious if inquired into: since the theory that woman should live by physical attraction of the opposite sex has never been seriously denied, but rather insisted upon, by men, upon what principle is solicitation, or open offer of such attraction, made a legal offence? (Not because the woman is a danger to the community, since the male sensualist is an equal source of danger.) Only, apparently, because the advance comes from the wrong side. I speak under correction, but cannot, unaided, light upon any other explanation; and mine seems to be borne out by the fact that, in other ranks of life, custom, like the above-mentioned law, strenuously represses any open advance on the part of the woman. So emphatic, indeed, is this unwritten law, that one cannot help suspecting that it was needful it should be emphatic, lest woman, adapting herself to her economic position, should take the initiative in a matter on which her livelihood depended, and deprive her employer not only of the pleasure of the chase, but of the illusion that their common bargain was as much a matter of romance and volition on her part as on his.

As a matter of fact, that law that the first advances must come from the side of the man is, as was only to be expected, broken, and broken every day; sometimes directly, but far more often indirectly. The woman bent on matrimony is constantly on the alert to evade its workings, conscious that in her attempt to do so she can nearly always count on the ready, if unspoken, co-operation of her sisters. This statement is, I know, in flat contravention of the firmly-rooted masculine belief that one woman regards another as an enemy to be depreciated consistently in masculine eyes, and that women spend their lives in one long struggle to gratify an uncontrollable desire for admiration at each other's expense. (I have myself been told by a man that he would never be so foolishly discourteous as to praise one woman in another's hearing. I, on my part, desirous also of being wisely courteous, did not attempt to shake the magnificent belief in his own importance to me which the statement betrayed.) Admiration is a very real passion in some women, as it is a very real passion in some men; but what, in women, is often mistaken for it is ambition, a desire to get on and achieve success in life in the only way in which it is open to a woman to achieve it — through the favour of man. Which is only another way of saying what I have insisted on before — that a good many feminine actions which are commonly and superficially attributed to sexual impulse have their root in the commercial instinct.

It is because women, consciously or unconsciously, recognise the commercial nature of the undertaking that they interest themselves so strongly in the business of matchmaking, other than their own. Men have admitted that interest, of course — the thing is too self-evident to be denied — and, as their manner is, attributed it to an exuberant sexuality which overflows on to its surroundings; steadfastly declining to take into account the 'professional' element in its composition, since that would necessarily imply the existence of an *esprit de corps* amongst women.

I myself cannot doubt that there does exist a spirit of practical, if largely unconscious, trade unionism in a class engaged in extracting, under many difficulties and by devious ways, its livelihood from the employer, man. (I need scarcely point out that man, like every other wage-payer, has done his level best and utmost to suppress the spirit of combination, and encourage distrust and division, amongst the wage-earners in the matrimonial market; and that the trade of marriage, owing to the isolation of the workers, has offered unexampled opportunities for such suppression of unity and encouragement of distrust and division.) But, in spite of this, women in general recognise the economic necessity of marriage for each other, and in a spirit of instinctive comradeship seek to forward it by every means in their power. There must be something extraordinarily and unnaturally contemptible about a woman who, her own bargain made and means of livelihood secured, will not help another to secure hers; and it is that motive, and not a rapturous content in their own unclouded destiny, not an unhesitating conviction that their lot has fallen in a fair ground, which makes of so many married women industrious and confirmed matchmakers. What has been termed the 'huge conspiracy of married women' is, in fact, nothing but a huge trade union whose members recognise the right of others to their bread. To my mind, one of the best proofs of the reality of this spirit of unconscious trade unionism among women is the existence of that other feminine conspiracy of silence which surrounds the man at whom a woman, for purely mercenary reasons, is making a 'dead set'. In such a case, the only women who will interfere and warn the intended victim will be his own relatives – a mother or a sister; others, while under no delusions as to the interested nature of the motives by which the pursuer is actuated, will hold their tongues, and even go so far as to offer facilities for the chase. They realise that their fellow has a right to her chance – that she must follow her trade as best she can, and would no more dream of giving her away than the average decent workman would dream of going to an employer and informing him that one of his mates was not up to his job and should, therefore, be discharged. In these emergencies a man must look to a man for help; the sympathies of the practical and unromantic sex will be on the other side.

I shall not deny, of course, that there is active and bitter competition amongst women for the favour not only of particular men, but of men in general; but, from what I have said already, it will be gathered that I consider that competition to be largely economic and artificial. Where it is economic, it is produced by the same cause which produces active and bitter competition in other branches of industry — the overcrowding of the labour market. Where it is artificial, as distinct from purely economic, it is produced by the compulsory concentration of energy on one particular object, and the lack of facilities for dispersing that energy in other directions. It is not the woman with an interest in life who spends her whole time in competing with her otherwise unoccupied sisters for the smiles of a man.

Four

Marriage being to them not only a trade, but a necessity, it must follow as the night the day that the acquirement of certain characteristics — the characteristics required by an average man in an average wife — has been rendered inevitable for women in general. There have, of course, always been certain exceptional men who have admired and desired certain exceptional and eccentric qualities in their wives; but in estimating a girl's chances of pleasing — on which depended her chances of success or a comfortable livelihood — these exceptions, naturally, were taken into but small account, and no specialisation in their tastes and desires was allowed for in her training. The aim and object of that training was to make her approximate to the standard of womanhood set up by the largest number of men; since the more widely she was admired the better were her chances of striking a satisfactory bargain. The taste and requirements of the average man of her class having been definitely ascertained, her training and education was carried on on the principle of cultivating those qualities which he was likely to admire, and repressing with an iron hand those qualities to which he was likely to take objection; in short, she was fitted for her trade by the discouragement of individuality and eccentricity and the persistent moulding of her whole nature into the form which the ordinary husband would desire it to take. Her education, unlike her brothers', was not directed towards self-development and the bringing out of natural capabilities, but towards pleasing some one else — was not for her own benefit, but for that of another person.

No one has better expressed the essential difference between the education of men and women than Mr John Burns in a speech delivered to the 'Children of the State' at the North Surrey District School on 13 February, 1909. Addressing the boys the President of the Local Government Board said, 'I want you to be happy craftsmen, because you are trained to be healthy men.' Addressing the girls he is reported to have used the following words:

'To keep house, cook, nurse and delight in making others happy is your mission, duty and livelihood.'

The boys are to be happy themselves; the girls are to make others happy. No doubt Mr Burns spoke sincerely; but is he not one of the 'others'? And it is well to note that the 'making of others happy' is not put before the girls as an ideal, but as a duty and means of livelihood. They are to be self-sacrificing as a matter of business — a commercial necessity. It is because man realises that self-sacrifice in woman is not a matter of free-will, but of necessity, that he gives her so little thanks for it. Her duty and means of livelihood is to make others happy — in other words, to please him.

Whether she was trained to be useful or useless that was the object of her up-bringing. Men in one class of society would be likely to require wives able to do rough house or field work; so to do rough house or field work she was trained. Men in another class of society would be likely to require of their wives an appearance of helpless fragility; and girls in that particular class were educated to be incapable of sustained bodily effort.

It is this fact — that their training was a training not in their own, but in some one else's requirements — which, to my thinking, makes women so infinitely more interesting to watch and to analyse than men. Interesting, I mean, in the sense of exciting. Practically every woman I know has two distinct natures: a real and an acquired; that which she has by right of birth and heritage, and that which she has been taught she ought to have — and often thinks that she has attained to. And it is quite impossible even for another woman, conscious of the same division of forces in herself, to forecast which of these two conflicting temperaments will come uppermost at a given moment.

The average man is a straightforward and simple-minded creature compared to the average woman, merely because he has been allowed to develop much more on his own natural lines. He has only one centre of gravity; the woman has two. To put it in plain English, he usually knows what he wants; she, much more often than not, does not know anything of the kind. She is under the impression that she wants certain things which she has been told from her earliest childhood, and is being told all the time, are the things she ought to want. That is as far as she can go with certainty. This also can be said with certainty: that her first requirement, whether she knows it or not, is the liberty to discover what she really does require.

Once a man's character is known and understood it can usually be predicted with a fair degree of accuracy how he will act in any particular crisis or emergency — say, under stress of strong emotion or temptation. With his sister, on the other hand, you can never foresee at what point artificiality will break down and nature take command; which makes it infinitely more difficult, however well you know her, to predict her course of action under the same circumstances. The woman whose whole existence, from early dawn to dewy eve, is regulated by a standard of manners imposed upon her from without, whose ideals are purely artificial and equally reflected, will suddenly, and at an unexpected moment, reveal another and fundamental side of her nature of which she herself has probably lived in entire ignorance. And on the other hand — so ingrained in us all has artificiality become — a woman of the independent type, with a moral standard and ideals of her own setting up, may, when the current of her life is swept out of its ordinary course by emergency or strong emotion, take refuge, just as suddenly and unexpectedly in words and actions that are palpably unnatural to her and inspired by an instilled idea of what, under the circumstances, a properly constituted woman ought to say or do. Faced with a difficulty through which her own experience does not serve to guide her, she falls back on convention and expresses the thoughts of others in the stilted language that convention has put into her mouth. I have known this happen more than once, and seen a real human being of flesh and blood suddenly and unconsciously transformed into one of those curious creatures, invented by male writers and called women for lack of any other name, whose sins and whose virtues alike are the sins and virtues considered by male writers to be suitable and becoming to the opposite sex.

For generation after generation the lives of women of even the slightest intelligence and individuality must have been one long and constant struggle between the forces of nature endeavouring to induce in them that variety which is another word for progress and their own enforced strivings to approximate to a single monotonous type — the type of the standard and ideal set up for them by man, which was the standard and ideal of his own comfort and enjoyment. However squarely uncompromising the characteristics of any given woman, the only vacant space for her occupation was round, and into the round hole she had to go. Were her soul the soul of a pirate, it had to be encased in a body which pursued the peaceful avocation of a cook. Even when she kicked over the traces and gave respectability the go-by, she could only do so after one particular and foregone fashion — a fashion encouraged if not openly approved by man. The male sinner might go to the devil in any way he chose; for her there was only one road to the nethermost hell, and, dependent even in this, she needed a man to set her feet upon the path. Her vices, like her virtues, were forced and stereotyped. They sprang from the same root; vice, with her, was simply an excess of virtue. Vicious or virtuous, matron or outcast, she was made and not born.

There must be many attributes and characteristics of the general run of women which are not really the attributes and characteristics of their sex, but of their class — a class persistently set apart for the duties of sexual attraction, house-ordering and the bearing of children. And the particular qualities that, in the eyes of man, fitted them for the fulfilment of these particular duties, generation after generation of women, whatever their natural temperament and inclination, have sought to acquire — or if not the actual qualities themselves, at least an outward semblance of them. Without some semblance of those qualities life would be barred to them.

There are very few women in whom one cannot, now and again, trace the line of cleavage between real and acquired, natural and class, characteristics. The same thing, of course, holds good of men, but in a far less degree since, many vocations being open to them, they tend naturally and on the whole to fall into the class for which temperament and inclination fit them. A man with a taste for an open-air life does not as a rule become a chartered accountant, a student does not take up deep-sea fishing as a suitable profession. But with women the endeavour to approximate to a single type has always been compulsory. It is ridiculous to suppose that nature, who never makes two blades of grass alike, desired to turn out indefinite millions of women all cut to the regulation pattern of wifehood: that is to say, all home-loving, charming, submissive, industrious, unintelligent, tidy, possessed with a desire to please, well-dressed, jealous of their own sex, self-sacrificing, cowardly, filled with a burning passion for maternity, endowed with a talent for cooking, narrowly uninterested in the world outside their own gates, and capable of sinking their own identity and interests in the interests and identity of a husband. I imagine that very few women naturally unite in their single persons these characteristics of the class wife; but, having been relegated from birth upwards to the class wife, they had to set to work, with or against the grain, to acquire some semblance of those that they knew were lacking.

There being no question of a line of least resistance for women, it is fairly obvious that the necessity (in many instances) of making a silk purse out of a sow's ear and instilling the qualities of tidiness, love of home, cowardice, unintelligence, etc., etc., into persons who were born with quite other capacities and defects must have resulted in a pitiable waste of good material, sacrificed upon the altar of a domesticity arranged in the interests of the husband. But infinitely worse in its effect upon womanhood in general was the insincerity which, in many cases, was the prime lesson and result of a girl's education and upbringing. I do not mean, of course, that the generality of girls were consciously, of set purpose, and in so many words taught to be insincere; but it seems fairly certain to me that generations of mothers have tacitly instructed their daughters to assume virtues (or the reverse) which they had not.

It could not be otherwise. Success in the marriage-market demanded certain qualifications; and, as a matter of economic and social necessity, if those qualifications were lacking, their counterfeit presentment was assumed. When helplessness and fragility were the fashion amongst wives, the girl-child who was naturally as plucky as her brothers was schooled into an affected and false timidity. Men were understood to admire and reverence the maternal instinct in women; so the girl who had no especial interest in children affected a mechanical delight in, petted, fondled and made much of them. (I myself have seen this done on more than one occasion; of course in the presence of men.) And — worst and most treacherous insincerity of all — since men were understood to dislike clever women, the girl who had brains, capacity, intellect, sought to conceal, denied possession of them, so that her future husband might enjoy, unchallenged, the pleasurable conviction of her mental inferiority to himself.

Of all the wrongs that have been inflicted upon woman there has been none like unto this — the enforced arrest of her mental growth — and none which bears more bitter and eloquent testimony to the complete and essential servility of her position. For her the eleventh commandment was an insult — 'Thou shalt not think'; and the most iniquitous condition of her marriage bargain this — that her husband, from the height of his self-satisfaction, should be permitted to esteem her a fool.

It was not only that, from one generation to another, woman was without encouragement to use her higher mental qualities — that her life was lacking in the stimulus of emulation so far as they were concerned, that her own particular trade made very few demands upon them. As if these things in themselves were not discouragement enough, she was directly forbidden to cultivate the small share of intellect she was understood to possess. Science was closed to her and art degraded to a series of 'parlour tricks.' It was not enough that she should be debarred from material possessions; from possessions that were not material, from the things of the spirit, she must be debarred as well. Nothing more plainly illustrates the fact that man has always regarded her as existing not for herself and for her own benefit, but for his use and pleasure solely. His use for her was the gratification of his own desire, the menial services she rendered without payment; his pleasure was in her flesh, not in her spirit; therefore the things of the spirit were not for her.

One wonders what it has meant for the race — this persistent desire of the man to despise his wife, this economic need of countless women to arrest their mental growth? It has amounted to this — that one of the principal qualifications for motherhood has been a low standard of intelligence. We hear a very great deal about the beauty and sanctity of motherhood; we might, for a change, hear something about the degradation thereof — which has been very real. To stunt one's brain in order that one may bear a son does not seem to me a process essentially sacred or noble in itself; yet millions of mothers have instructed their daughters in foolishness so that they, in their turn, might please, marry and beget children. Most of those daughters, no doubt — humanity being in the main slothful and indifferent — endured the process with equanimity; but there must always have been some, and those not the least worthy, who suffered piteously under the systematic thwarting of definite instincts and vague ambitions. In every generation there must have been women who desired life at first hand, and in whom the crushing of initiative and inquiry and the substitution of servile for independent qualities, must have caused infinite misery. In every generation there must have been women who had something to give to those who lived outside the narrowing walls of their home; and who were not permitted to give it. They soured and stifled; but they were not permitted to give it.

But, after all, the suffering of individual women under the law of imposed stupidity is a very small thing compared with the effect of that law upon humanity as a whole. The sex which reserved to itself the luxury of thinking appears to have been somewhat neglectful of its advantages in that respect, since it failed to draw the obvious conclusion that sons were the sons of their mothers as well as of their fathers. Yet it is a commonplace that exceptional men are born of exceptional women — that is to say, of women in whom the natural instinct towards self-expansion and self-expression is too strong to be crushed and thwarted out of existence by the law of imposed stupidity.

That law has reacted inevitably upon those who framed and imposed it; since it is truth and not a jest that the mission in life of many women has been to suckle fools — of both sexes. Women have been trained to be unintelligent breeding-machines until they have become unintelligent breeding-machines — how unintelligent witness the infant death-rate from improper feeding. Judging by that and other things, the process of transforming the natural woman into flesh without informing spirit would appear, in a good many instances, to have been attended by a fair amount of success. In some classes she still breeds brainlessly. That is what she is there for, not to think of the consequences. Has she not been expressly forbidden to think? If she is a failure as a wife and mother, it is because she is nothing else. And those of us who are now alive might be better men and women, seeing more light where now we strive and slip in darkness, if our fathers had not insisted so strongly and so steadfastly upon their right to despise the women they made their wives — who were our mothers.

I have said that this condemnation to intellectual barrenness is the strongest proof of the essential servility of woman's position in the eyes of man, and I repeat that statement. It cannot be repeated too often. So long as you deprive a human being of the right to make use of its own mental property, so long do you keep that human being in a state of serfdom. You may disguise the fact even from yourself by an outward show of deference and respect, the lifting of a hat or the ceding of a pathway; but the fact remains. Wherever and whenever man has desired to degrade his fellow and tread him under foot, he has denied him, first of all, the right to think, the means of education and inquiry. Every despotism since the world began has recognised that it can only work in secret — that its ways must not be known. No material tyranny can hope to establish itself firmly and for long unless it has at its disposal the means to establish also a tyranny that is spiritual and intellectual. When you hold a man's mind in thrall you can do what you will with his body; you possess it and not he. Always those who desired power over their fellows have found it a sheer necessity to possess their bodies through their souls; and for this reason, when you have stripped a man of everything except his soul, you have to go on and strip him of that too, lest, having it left to him, he asks questions, ponder the answers and revolt. In all ages the aim of a despotism, small or great, material or intellectual, has been to keep its subjects in ignorance and darkness; since, in all ages, discontent and rebellion have come with the spread of knowledge, light and understanding. So soon as a human being is intelligent enough to doubt and frame the question, 'Why is this?' he can no longer be satisfied with the answer, 'Because I wish it.' That is an answer which inevitably provokes the rejoinder, 'But I do not' — which is the essence and foundation of heresy and high treason.

Those in high places — that is to say, those who desired power over others — have, as a condition of their existence in high places, fought steadfastly against the spread of the means of enlightenment. No right has been more bitterly denied than the right of a man to think honestly and to communicate his thoughts to his fellows. Persons who claimed that right have been at various times (and for the edification of other persons who might be tempted to go and do likewise) stoned, devoured by wild beasts, excommunicated, shut up in dungeons, burned at the stake and hanged, drawn and quartered. In spite, however, of these drastic penalties — and other lesser ones too numerous to mention — there has always been a section of humanity which has stubbornly persisted, even at the risk of roasting or dismemberment, in thinking its own thoughts on some particular subject and saying what they were. To persons of this frame of mind it probably did not much matter how soon they had done with an existence which they had to look at through other people's eyes and talk about in suitable phrases arranged for them by other people. So they risked the penalty and said what they wanted to. The history of the world has been a succession of demands, more or less spasmodic, more or less insistent, on the part of subjected classes, nations and sects, to be allowed to see things in their own way and with an eye to their own interests, spiritual or material. Which is why a free press and a free pulpit have often seemed worth dying for.

Wherever civilisation exists various classes, sects and nations of men have, one by one, claimed the right to that examination of things for themselves which is called education. They have never attained to it without opposition; and one of the most frequent and specious forms of that opposition is embodied in the argument that education would not only be useless to them, but would unfit them for their duties. No doubt this argument was often put forward in all honesty as the outcome of a conviction that was none the less sincere because it was prompted by self-interest. That conviction had its roots in the common and widespread inability to realise the actual human identity of other persons — in the habit of summing them up and estimating them in the light only of the salient (and often superficial) characteristics which affect ourselves. I can best explain what I mean by saying that to many of us the word 'clerk' does not summon up the mental representation of an actual man who spends some of his time writing, but of something in the shape of a man that is continuously occupied in driving a pen. In other words, we lose sight of the man himself in one of his attributes; and the same with a miner, a sailor, etc. Thus to the persons in high places who opposed the education of the agricultural labourer, the agricultural labourer was not an actual man, but a hoe or a harrow in human shape; and they were quite honestly and logically unable to see what this animated implement of agricultural toil could want with the inside of a book. Practically, however, they were denying humanity to the labourer and sinking his identity in one particular quality — the physical capacity for field-work.

This, as I have explained elsewhere, is the manner in which woman, as a rule, is still regarded — not as a human being with certain physical and mental qualities which enable her to bring children into the world and cook a dinner, but as a breeding-machine and the necessary adjunct to a frying-pan. So regarded, independence of thought and anything beyond a very limited degree of mental cultivation are unnecessary to her, even harmful, since they might possibly result in the acquirement of other attributes quite out of place in the adjunct to a frying-pan.

Five

With the advance of civilisation one subject class after another has risen in revolt, more or less violent, more or less peaceful, and asserted its right to inquire, to think in its own way — that is to say, it has asserted its humanity. But it is a proof of my statement that woman has never been regarded as fully human, that the successive classes of men who have, in turn, asserted their own humanity have totally forgotten to assert hers, have left her, whatever her rank, in a class apart, and continued to treat her as a domestic animal whose needs were only the needs of a domestic animal.

The aristocratic instinct is by no means confined to those born in the purple. (Some of the most startlingly aristocratic sentiments I have ever heard came from the lips of persons believed by themselves to entertain ultra-democratic ideas.) The sense of power over others is just as attractive to the many as it is to the few; and thus it has happened that men, in every class, have taken a pleasure in the dependence and subjection of their womenfolk, and, lest their power over them should be undermined, have refused to their womenfolk the right to think for themselves. The essential cruelty of that refusal they disguised from themselves by explaining that women could not think even if they tried. We have all heard the definition of woman — episcopal, I think — as a creature who cannot reason and pokes the fire from the top.

This disbelief in the existence of reasoning powers in woman is still, it seems to me, a very real thing — at least, I have run up against it a good many times in the course of my life, and I do not suppose that I am an exception in that respect. And the really interesting thing about this contemptuous attitude of mind is that it has led to the adoption, by those who maintain it, of a very curious subterfuge. It is, of course, quite impossible to deny that a woman's mind does go through certain processes which control and inspire her actions and conclusions — sometimes very swiftly and effectively; but to these mental processes, which in men are called reason, they give, in woman, the title of intuition.

Now the word 'intuition', when used in connection with woman, conveys to the average male mind a meaning closely akin to that of the word instinct — as opposed to reason. (In this insistence on the instinctive character of our mental processes the average man is, of course, quite consistent; since he imagines that we exist only for the gratification of two instincts, the sexual and the maternal, it does not seem unreasonable on his part to conclude that we also think by instinct.) I am certain that I am right as to this masculine habit of confusing intuition with instinct; since on every occasion on which I have been more or less politely — but always firmly — informed that I had no intellect, but could console myself for the deficiency by the reflection that I possessed the usual feminine quality of intuition, I have made a point of bringing the person who made the remark to book by insisting upon an exact definition of the term. In every single case within my own experience the exact definition — as I have been careful to point out — has been not insight, but instinct. Our mental processes, in short, are supposed to be on the same level as the mental process which starts the newly-hatched gosling on its waddle to the nearest pond. We are supposed to know what we want without knowing why we want it — just like the gosling, which does not make a bee-line for the water because it has carefully examined its feet, discovered that they are webbed, and drawn the inference that webbed feet are suitable for progress in water.

This question of the intuitive or instinctive powers of woman is one that has always interested me extremely; and as soon as I realised that my mind was supposed to work in a different way from a man's mind, and that I was supposed to arrive at conclusions by a series of disconnected and frog-like jumps, I promptly set to work to discover if that was really the case by the simple expedient of examining the manner in which I did arrive at conclusions. I believe that (on certain subjects, at any rate) I think more rapidly than most people — which does not mean, of course, that I think more correctly. It does mean, however, that I very often have to explain to other people the process by which I have arrived at my conclusions (which might otherwise appear intuitive); therefore I may be called a good subject for investigation. I can honestly say that I have never been at a loss for such an explanation. I can trace the progress of my thought, step by step, just as a man can trace his. I may reason wrongly, but I do not reason in hops. And I have yet to meet the woman who does. I have met many women who were in the habit of coming to conclusions that were altogether ridiculous and illogical; but they were conclusions — drawn from insufficient data — and not guesses. No sane human being regulates — or does not regulate — its life, as we are supposed to do, by a series of vague and uncontrolled guesses.

I imagine that the idea that women do so control their lives must have had its origin in the fact that men and women usually turn their mental energy into entirely different channels. On subjects that are familiar to us we think quickly, and acquire a mental dexterity akin to the manual dexterity of a skilled artisan. But the subjects upon which women exercise this mental dexterity are not, as a rule, the same as those upon which men exercise theirs; the latter have usually left narrow social and domestic matters alone, and it is in narrow social and domestic matters that we are accustomed to think quickly. We are swifter than they are, of course, at drawing the small inferences from which we judge what a man will like or dislike; but then, for generations the business of our lives has been to find out what a man will like or dislike, and it would be rather extraordinary if we had not, in the course of ages, acquired in it a measure of that rapid skill which in any other business would be called mechanical, but in ours is called intuitive.

This theory of intuition or instinct, then, I take, as I have already said, to be in the nature of a subterfuge on the part of the male — a sop to his conscience, and a plausible excuse for assuming that we have not the intelligence which (if it were once admitted that we possessed it) we should have the right to cultivate by independent thinking. But to admit the right of a human being to independent thinking is also to admit something else far more important and unpleasant — his right to sit in judgment upon you. That right every despotism that ever existed has steadily denied to its subjects; therefore, there is nothing extraordinary in the fact that man has steadily denied it to woman. He has always preferred that she should be too ignorant to sit in judgment upon him, punishing her with ostracism if she was rash enough to attempt to dispel her own ignorance. One of her highest virtues, in his eyes, was a childish and undeveloped quality about which he threw a halo of romance when he called it by the name of innocence. So far has this insistence on ignorance or innocence in a wife been carried, that even in these days many who marry young have but a very vague idea of what they are doing; while certain risks attaching to the estate of marriage are, in some ranks of life at any rate, sedulously concealed from them as things which it is unfit for them to know.

It is a subject that is both difficult and unpleasant to touch upon; but while it will always be unpleasant, it ought not to be difficult, and I should be false to my beliefs if I apologised for touching upon it. Women, like men, when they enter upon a calling, have a perfect right to know exactly what are the dangers and drawbacks attached to their calling; you do not, when you turn a man into a pottery or a dynamite factory, sedulously conceal from him the fact that there are such things as lead-poisoning or combustion. On the contrary, you warn him — as women are seldom warned. I have been astonished at the number of women I have met who seem to have hardly more than a vague inkling — and some not even that — of the tangible, physical consequence of loose living.

I have not the faintest intention of indicting a sermon on masculine morals. If the average man chooses to dispense with morals as we understand them, that is his affair and a matter for his own conscience; if he is so constituted physically that he cannot live as we do, and has practically no choice in the matter, that is his misfortune. But I do say this: that the average woman has a perfect right to know what are the results of loose living in so far as those results may affect her and her children. If marriage is a trade we ought to know its risks — concerning which there exists a conspiracy of silence. Is the cause to which I have alluded ever mentioned, except in technical publications, in connection with the infant death-rate?

Those of us who have discovered that there are risks attaching to the profession of marriage other than the natural ones of child birth, have very often made the discovery by accident — which ought not to be. I made the discovery in that way myself while I was still very young — by the idle opening of a book which, because it was a book, was a thing to be opened and looked into. I was puzzled at first, and then the thing stared me in the face — a simple matter of bald statement and statistics. I remember the thought which flashed into my mind — we are told we have got to be married, but we are never told *that!* It was my first conscious revolt against the compulsory nature of the trade of marriage.

Six

This insistent and deliberate stunting of woman's intellectual growth is, as I have already stated, the best proof of her essentially servile position in the household; and that being the case, it is not to be wondered at that her code of honour and morals is essentially a servile code. That is to say, its origin and guiding motive is the well-being, moral and material, of some one else. Like her stupidity woman's morality has been imposed on her, and to a great extent is not morality at all, in the proper sense of the word, but a code of manners formulated in the interests of her master.

I wish to make it clear that when I speak of morality in this connection I am not using the word in the narrow sense in which it is sometimes employed. By a standard of morality I mean a rule of life which we adopt as a guide to our conduct, and endeavour, more or less successfully, to apply to every action — to our dealings with others as well as to our dealings with our own hearts.

I cannot better explain what I mean by the essential servility of woman's code of morals than by quoting Milton's well-known line: 'He for God only, she for God in him.'

That one brief verse condenses into a nutshell the difference in the moral position of the two sexes — expresses boldly, simply, straightforwardly, the man's belief that he had the right to divert and distort the moral impulse and growth in woman to serve his own convenience. No priesthood has ever made a claim more arrogant than this claim of man to stand between woman and her God, and divert the spiritual forces of her nature into the channel that served him best. The real superiority of man consists in this: that he is free to obey his conscience and to serve his

God — if it be in him so to do. Woman is not. She can serve Him only at second hand — can obey His commands not directly but only by obeying the will of the man who stands between her and the Highest, and who has arrogated to himself not merely the material control of her person and her property, but the spiritual control of her conscience.

This is no fanciful piece of imagery. These are laws still in existence — laws of an earlier age — which prove how complete has been this moral control which we are only now shaking off, since they presume a man's entire responsibility for the actions of his wife, be those actions good or ill. That a woman at her husband's bidding should bend her conscience to his will as a reed bends; that, because he desired it of her, she should break and defy every commandment of God and man; this seemed to our forefathers a natural thing, and a course of action befitting her station and place in life. So far from blaming, they condoned it in her and have expressed that view of the matter in their law — sometimes with awkward and annoying results for a later generation. Woman, until she began to feel in herself the stirrings of independence — woman, when she was just the wife-and-mother-and-nothing-else, the domestic animal — seems to me to have been a creature whom you could not have described as being either moral or immoral. She was just unmoral. Whether she did good or evil was not, as far as her own individuality went, of very much account since the standard set up for her was not of her own setting up; it had been erected for the comfort and well-being of her master. Her virtues were second-hand virtues, instilled into her for the convenience of another; and she did what was right in his eyes, not in her own, after the manner of a child. Therefore she was neither moral nor immoral, but servile. The motive which guided and impelled her from childhood was a low one — the desire (disinterestedly or for her own advantage) of pleasing some one else. (To make others happy, as Mr Burns expresses it.) The desire to please being the motive power of her existence, her code of honour and ethics was founded not on thought, conviction or even natural impulse, but on observation of the likes and dislikes of those she had to please. Hence its extraordinary and inconsistent character, its obvious artificiality and the manifest traces it bears of having been imposed upon her from without. For instance, no natural ethical code emanating from within could have summed up woman's virtue in *a* virtue − physical purity. That confusion of one virtue with virtue in general was certainly of masculine origin arising from the masculine habit of thinking of woman only in connection with her relations to himself. To other aspects of her life and character man was indifferent − they hardly existed for him. And of masculine origin, too, was that extraordinary article of the code by which it was laid down that a woman's 'honour' was, to all intents and purposes, a matter of chance − a thing which she only possessed because no unkind fate had thrown her in the way of a man sufficiently brutal to deprive her of it by force. Her honour, in short, was not a moral but a physical quality.

One sees, of course, the advantage from the male point of view, of this peculiar provision of the code. In a world where the pickpocket class had the upper hand a somewhat similar regulation would, no doubt, be in force; and it would be enacted, by a custom stronger than law, that to have one's pocket picked was in itself a disgrace which must on no account be cried aloud upon the housetops or communicated to the police. To reveal and publish the fact that your purse had been snatched from you by force would be to make yourself a mark for scorn and for hissing, to bring upon yourself an obloquy far greater than that accorded to the active partner in the transaction, whose doings would be greeted with a shrug of the shoulders and the explanation that pickpockets are pickpockets, and will never be anything but what nature has made them; and, after all, you must have dangled the purse temptingly before his eyes. Under these circumstances, with the thief at liberty to ply his trade, the fact that you had money in your pocket would be, strictly speaking, an accident; and, to make the parallel complete, the lack of your money − the fact that it had been taken from you even against your will − would have to be accounted a black disgrace, leaving a lasting smear upon your whole life. That, it seems to me, is the exact position with regard to what is commonly termed a woman's 'honour'. I should prefer to put it that a woman has no honour; only an accident.

In such a world as I have described − a world run in the interest of the light-fingered class − the average and decent man would find it just as easy and just as difficult to take legal proceedings against the person who had violently deprived him of his purse as the average and decent woman would now find it were she to take legal proceedings against the man who had violently deprived her of her honour. Nominally, of course, justice would afford him a fair hearing and the process of law would be at his disposal; actually he would make himself a target for contempt and scorn, and the very men who tried his case, with every desire to be unbiassed, would be prejudiced against him because he had not hidden his disgrace in silence. In most cases the effect of such a public opinion would be to make him hold his tongue, and practically by his silence become an abettor and accomplice in the offence wrought upon himself and by which he himself had suffered. He might, if his mould were sensitive, choose the river rather than exposure – as women have done before now.

Honour, as I understand it, is not physical or accidental; is not even reputation, which is a species of reflection of honour in the minds of others; it is a state of mind resulting from a voluntary and conscious adherence to certain rules of life and conduct. As such it is entirely your own possession and creation, a thing of which no one can rob you but yourself; it is at no man's mercy but your own. It is because woman, as a rule, has not possessed the power of giving voluntary and conscious adherence to rules of life and conduct, because the rules of life and conduct which she follows have been framed in the interests of others and forced upon her in the interests of others – that she has been denied any other than a purely physical and accidental 'honour'.

One's mind goes back to two children in the school-room pondering seriously and in the light of their own unaided logic the puzzling story of Lucrece – much expurgated and newly acquired during the course of a Roman history lesson. The expurgated Roman history book had made it clear that she was a woman greatly to be admired; we sat with knitted brows and argued why. Something had been done to her – we were vague as to the nature of the something, but had gathered from the hurried manner of our instructress that here was a subject on which you must not ask for precise information. Our ignorance baffled and aggrieved us since fuller knowledge might have thrown light upon an otherwise incomprehensible case. Something had been done to her by a wicked man and against her will — so much we knew. She had tried all she could to prevent it, but he was the stronger — the expurgated Roman history had said, 'By force'. Therefore, whatever had happened was not her fault. Yet the next morning she had sent post-haste for her husband and her father, told them all about it and stabbed herself to the heart before their eyes! Try as we would to sympathise with this paragon of Roman virtue, the action seemed inconsequent. It implied remorse where remorse was not only unnecessary but impossible. If she had stabbed Sextus Tarquinius, or if Sextus Tarquinius had stabbed himself in a fit of repentance for his own mysterious ill-doing . . . . But why needlessly distress your family by descending into an early grave because some one else had been mysteriously wicked while you yourself had done no harm at all? Our sense of logic and justice was shaken to its foundations. The verdict of admiration recorded in the history book stared us in the face, conflicting with our own conclusions; and it was our reverence for the written word alone that prevented the open and outspoken judgment, 'She was silly'.

So two small persons, to whom sex was still a matter of garments, seriously troubled by their own inability to appreciate a virtue held up to them for reverence, with views as yet level and unwarped on the subject of justice, and still in complete ignorance of the 'economic' law that the cost of sin, like the cost of taxation, is always shifted on to the shoulders of those least able to bear or to resent it.

The key to the curious and inferior position of woman with regard to breaches, voluntary or involuntary, of the moral law is to be found in this right of the strongest to avoid payment. It is a right that is recognised and openly acted upon in the world of business and of property, that has to be considered and taken into account by financiers and statesmen in the collection of revenue and the imposition of taxes. It is the general exercise of this right that makes the incidence of taxation a study for experts. Roughly its result is, the weakest pays. Tax the business man and he will set to work to send up prices, collecting his additional toll in farthings, pence and shillings from his customers, or to save it by cutting down the wages of his employees. Tax the landlord, and he sends up rents — perhaps in the slums.

The stronger the position of the capitalist, the more easily does he avoid payment. If his position is so strong that he is an actual monopolist he can avoid it with complete ease, simply taking the amount required from the pockets of those who are unable to refuse his demands, handing it over to the powers that be and paying himself for his trouble in doing so.

The incidence of blame in offences against the code which regulated the sexual relations of men and women is governed by laws similar to those which govern the incidence of taxation. The stronger party to the offence, taking advantage of his strength, has refused to pay; has simply and squarely declined to take his share of the mutual punishment, and has shifted a double portion thereof on to the shoulders of the weaker party. So far as I can see that is the real and only reason for the preferential treatment of man under the moral code — a preferential treatment insisted upon by Adam in the garden of Eden when he anxiously explained to the Deity that the woman was to blame, and insisted upon ever since by his descendants. Is it not Adam who sniggers over spicy stories at his club, retails them to the wife of his bosom and then gives vent to manly and generous indignation at the expense of the spinster who repeats them at third hand? while the extreme reluctance of a purely male electorate to raise what is termed the age of consent in girls is perhaps the most striking example of this tendency of the stronger to shift the responsibility of his misdeeds on to any shoulders but his own — even on to the shoulders of a child.

Palpable and obvious hardship dealt out by men to women is usually defended, if not explained, by that more or less vague reference to natural law, which is again an attempt to shift responsibility; and I have heard the position of woman as scapegoat for the sins of the man justified by her greater importance to the race as the mother of the next generation. This position of trust and responsibility, it is urged, makes her fall more blameworthy in itself, since her offence is not only an offence against her own person. One would feel more inclined to give ear to this explanation if it could be proved that it was only in the case of actual infractions of the moral code that the male was in the habit of availing himself of his opportunities of shifting the blame that should be his on to the back of the weaker vessel. But it is

61

not. Why, for instance, when a man who has been engaged to a woman changes his mind and throws her over against her will should the woman be regarded as to some extent humiliated and disgraced by the action of another person, an action over which she has had no control whatever, which has, in fact, been performed against her express desire? Yet in such circumstances the woman who has been left in the lurch is supposed to suffer, quite apart from the damage to her affection, a sort of moral damage and disgrace from the heartlessness or fickleness of another person — the man to whom she has been engaged; and this moral damage is, I believe, taken into account in actions for breach of promise of marriage (where there is no question of seduction). In these instances of fickleness on the side of the one party to the engagement, there is no suggestion of guilt or offence in the other party — the woman; yet the consequences of guilt and offence have been transferred to her shoulders, simply, it seems to me, because the guilty and offending party, being the stronger, declined to bear them himself. And woman's code of honour and morals being essentially a servile code, designed for the benefit of those in authority over her, she accepts the position without protest and takes shame to herself for the fault of another person. The first provision of a wider code — a code drawn up by herself — must be that she will only accept responsibility for her own actions. Until she has taken her stand on that principle she cannot hope for a freedom that is real, even a material freedom. At present her position, in this respect, is analogous to that of the mediaeval whipping-boy or those slaves of antiquity who were liable to be put to death for the sins of their masters — a position entirely incompatible with the most elementary ideas of liberty and justice. The chaste and virtuous Lucrece whose untimely fate so distraught our youthful brains was not so much the victim of one man's evil passions and wrong-doing as of her own servile code of morals; she was (if she ever existed) a slave of undoubted and heroic virtue — but certainly a slave and not a free woman, accountable for her own acts and her own acts alone.

As a matter of fact, if we come to look into them closely, we find that the virtues that have been enjoined upon woman for generations are practically all servile virtues — the virtues a man desires in and enjoins upon those whom he wishes to hold in subjection. Honour, in the proper sense of the word, truth-telling, independence of thought and action, self-reliance and courage are the qualities of a free people; and, because they are the qualities of a free people, they have not been required of her. Submission, suppleness, coaxing manners, a desire to please and ingratiate, tact and a capacity for hard work for which no definite return is to be expected, are the qualities encouraged in a servile or subject race by those in authority over them; and it is precisely these qualities which have been required of woman. The ordinary male ideal of a mother is a servile ideal — a person who waits on others, gives way to others, drudges for others, and only lives for the convenience of others. The ordinary male ideal of a wife is a servile ideal — a person with less brains than himself, who is pleasant to look at, makes him comfortable at home and respects his authority. And it is the unfortunate fact that she is expected to live down to this ideal — and very often does — which accounts for that frequent phenomenon, the rapid mental deterioration of the woman who has fulfilled her destiny and attained to a completeness that is synonymous with stagnation.

It is obvious that marriage — the companionship of two reasonable human beings — ought not, under natural conditions, to have a stupefying effect upon one of the parties to the arrangement; and, as far as I can see, where the woman is recognised as a responsible human being with an individuality and interests of her own, and with a right to her own opinion, it does not have that effect. The professional woman — a class which I know fairly well — is not, as a rule, less interesting and individual after marriage than before it, simply because she does not usually marry the type of man who would expect her to swamp her own ideas and personality in his; and the working woman of another class, who, as the manager and financier of the household, is obliged to keep her wits sharp, is often an extremely interesting person with a shrewd and characteristic outlook on life. It is the woman of the 'comfortable' class, with narrow duties and a few petty responsibilities, who now-a-days most readily conforms to the servile type of manners and morals set up for her admiration and imitation, sinks into a nonentity or a busy-body, and does her best to gratify and justify her husband's predilection for regarding her mental capacity with contempt.

Seven

One peculiarity of the trade at which so many women earn their livelihood I have, as yet, hardly touched upon. It is this: that however arduous and exacting the labour that trade entails — and the rough manual work of most households is done by women — it is not paid except by a wage of subsistence. There may be exceptions, of course, but, as a general rule, the work done by the wife and mother in the home is paid for merely by supplying her with the necessaries of existence — food, lodging, and clothing. She is fed and lodged on the same principle as a horse is fed and lodged — so that she may do her work, her cooking, her cleaning, her sewing, and the tending and rearing of her children. She may do it very well or she may do it very badly; but beyond food, lodging, and a certain amount of clothing, she can claim no wage for it. In short, her work in the home is not recognised either by the State or by the individual citizen (except in occasional instances) as work which has any commercial value.

There must, of course, be some reason why such intrinsically important work as the rearing of children and ministering to the comfort of the community should be held in such poor esteem that it is paid for at the lowest possible rate — subsistence rate. (Which means, of course, that wages in that particular branch of work have been forced just as low as they can go, since human beings cannot continue to exist without the means of supporting life.) And the principal reason for this state of things I take to be the compulsory nature of the trade. Given a sufficiently large number of persons destined and educated from birth for one particular calling, with no choice at all in the matter, and with every other calling and means of livelihood sternly barred to them, and you have all the conditions necessary for the forcing down of wages to the lowest possible point to which they will go — subsistence point. In that calling labour will be as cheap as the heart of the employer could desire; and incidentally it will tend to become what ill-paid labour always tends to become — inefficient. Exactly the same condition of affairs would prevail in any other trade — mining or boiler-making, for instance — if immense numbers of boys were brought up to be miners or boiler-makers, and informed that whatever their needs or desires, or whatever the state of the labour market in those particular callings, they could not turn their abilities into any other direction. Under those circumstances miners and boiler-makers would probably work for their keep and nothing more, as the ordinary wife has to do.

I shall be told, of course, that the position of a husband is not that of an ordinary employer of labour, and that the financial relations of a man and his wife are complicated by considerations of affection and mutual interest which make it quite impossible to estimate the exact wage-earning value of the wife's services in the household, or the price which she receives for them in other things than money. Even if, for the sake of argument, this be admitted as a general rule, it does not invalidate my point, which is that the compulsory nature of woman's principal trade is quite sufficient, in itself, to account for the fact that the workers in that trade are not deemed worthy of anything more than a wage of subsistence. Considerations of sentiment and affection may help to keep her direct monetary remuneration down; but to bring it down in the first instance nothing more was needed than compulsory over-crowding of the 'domestic service' market.

That the wage of subsistence — the board, lodging, and clothing — dealt out to a married woman is often board, lodging, and clothing on a very liberal and comfortable scale, does not alter the fact that it is essentially a wage of subsistence, regulated by the idea of what is necessary for subsistence in the particular class to which she may happen to belong. The plutocrat who wishes his wife to entertain cannot habitually feed her on fish and chips from round the corner, or renew her wardrobe in an old-clothes shop. But she does not get twelve-course dinners and dresses from the Rue de la Paix because she has earned them by extra attention to her duties as a wife and mother, but because they are necessary qualifications for the place in his household which her husband wishes her to take — because, without them, she could not fulfil the duties that he requires of her. The monetary reward of wifehood and motherhood depends entirely on the life, the good luck and the good nature of another person; the strictest attention to duty on the part of a wife and mother is of no avail without that. The really hard labour of housework and rearing children is done in those households where the wage of subsistence is lowest; and the women who receive most money from their husbands are precisely those who pass on the typical duties of a wife and mother to other persons — housekeepers, cooks, nurses, and governesses. Excellence in the trade is no guarantee of reward, which is purely a matter of luck; work, however hard, will not bring about that measure of independence, more or less comparative, which is attained by successful work in other trades. Dependence, in short, is the essence of wifehood as generally understood by the masculine mind.

Under normal and favourable conditions, then, a married woman without private means of her own obtains a wage of subsistence for the fulfilment of the duties required of her in her husband's household. Under unfavourable (but not very abnormal) conditions she does not even obtain that. In the case of the large army of married women who support idle or invalid husbands by paid labour outside the home, the additional work inside the home is carried on gratis, and without a suggestion of payment of any kind.

I am inclined to believe that the principle that payment should be made for domestic service rendered does not really enter into the question of a wife's wages; that those wages (of subsistence) are paid simply for the possession of her person, and that the other arts and accomplishments she may possess are not supposed to have any exchange value. At any rate, a mistress, from whom the domestic arts are not expected, is often just as expensively kept as a wife — which seems to point to my conclusion. What Mr John Burns has called a woman's 'duty and livelihood' is, in the strict sense of the term, not her livelihood at all. Her livelihood, as an ordinary wife, is a precarious dependence upon another person's life; should that other person die, she could not support herself and her children by remaining in 'woman's sphere' — cooking, tending the house, and looking after her young family. That sort of work having no commercial value, she and her young family would very shortly starve. The profession of the prostitute is a livelihood; the profession of the wife and mother is not. A woman can support her children by prostitution; she cannot do so by performing the duties ordinarily associated with motherhood.

That marriage has another side than the economic I should be the last to deny, as I should be the last to deny that there are many households in which subjection and dependence in the wife is not desired by her husband — households in which there is a sharing of material, as well as of intellectual, interests. But that does not alter the fact that the position of a great many other married women is simply that of an unpaid domestic servant on the premises of a husband. The services that, rendered by another, would command payment, or at least thanks, from her are expected as a matter of course. They are supposed to be natural to her; she is no more to be paid for them than she is to be paid for breathing or feeling hungry. (One wonders why it should be 'natural' in woman to do so many disagreeable things. Does the average man really believe that she has an instinctive and unquenchable craving for all the unpleasant and unremunerative jobs? or is that only a polite way of expressing his deeply-rooted conviction that when once she has got a husband she ought to be so thoroughly happy that a little dirty work more or less really cannot matter to her?)

It may be argued that in the greater number of cases marriage, for the husband, means the additional labour and expense of supporting a wife and children; and that this added labour and expense is expected from him as a matter of course, and that neither does he receive any thanks for it. Quite so; but, as I pointed out at the beginning of this book, marriage is a voluntary matter on the part of a man. He does not earn his living by it; he is under no necessity to undertake its duties and responsibilities should he prefer not to do so. He has other interests in life, and no social stigma attaches to him if he does not take to himself a wife and beget children. He enters the marriage state because he wishes to enter it, and is prepared to make certain necessary sacrifices in order to maintain a wife and family; whereas the position of the woman is very different. She very often enters the married state because she has to — because more lucrative trades are barred to her, because to remain unmarried will be to confess failure. This state of things in itself gives the man an advantage, and enables him to ensure (not necessarily consciously) that his share of the bargain shall be advantageous to himself — to ensure, in short, that he gets his money's worth. With his wife, on the other hand, it has often been a case of take it or leave it; since she knows that, if she does leave it, she will not be able to strike any more advantageous bargain elsewhere.

These being the conditions under which, consciously or unconsciously, the average wife strikes her bargain, it follows that in the ensuing division of labour she generally gets the worst of the transaction, the duties assigned to her being those which her husband would prefer not to perform. They are handed over to her as a matter of course, and on the assumption that they enter into what is commonly known as her 'sphere'. And it is this principle — that woman's work is the kind of work which man prefers not to do — which regulates and defines not only the labour of woman in her own household, but the labour of women generally.

I am quite aware that this principle is not openly admitted in assigning to woman her share of the world's work — that, on the contrary, the results of its application are explained away on the theory that there is a 'natural' division of labour between the two sexes. But when one comes to examine that theory, dispassionately and without prejudice, one finds that it does not hold water — or very little — since the estimate of woman's 'natural' work is such an exceedingly variable quantity. One nation, people, or class, will esteem it 'natural' in woman to perform certain duties which, in another nation, people, or class, are entirely left to men — so much so, that woman's sphere, like morality, seems to be defined by considerations 'purely geographical'. Unless we grasp the underlying principle that woman's 'natural' labour in any given community is the form of labour which the men of that community do not care to undertake, her share in the world's work must appear to be regulated by sheer and arbitrary chance.

Eight

As soon as one comes to examine this subject of the 'natural' sphere of woman and woman's work with anything like an open mind, one discovers that in at least nine cases out of ten the word 'suitable' or 'artificial' must be substituted for the word 'natural'. There are only two kinds of work natural to any human being: the labour by which, in fulfilment of the curse laid upon Adam, he needs to earn his bread; and what may be called the artistic or spontaneous labour which he puts of his own free will into his hobbies, his pleasures, and his interests. In some cases the two kinds — the bread-winning and the artistic or spontaneous form of labour — can be combined; and those who can so combine them, be they rich or poor, are the fortunate ones of the earth. To a person in actual need of the means of supporting existence any form of labour by which he or she can earn or obtain those means of existence is a perfectly natural one. A sufficiently hungry coal-heaver would do his best to hem stitch a silk pocket-handkerchief for the price of a meal, and a sufficiently hungry woman would wrestle with a coal-heaver's job for the same consideration. In neither case could the action of the sufficiently hungry person be called unnatural; on the contrary, it would be prompted by the first and most urgent of natural laws — the law of self-preservation, which would over-ride any considerations of unsuitability. It does not, of course, follow from this example that certain forms of labour are not more suitable to women in general, and others not more suitable to men in general; all I wish to insist on is that suitable and natural are not interchangeable terms, and that what may be suitable at one place and under one set of conditions may not be suitable in another place and under another set of conditions.

The care of young children seems to be a department of labour so suitable to women that one may venture to assume that it is natural to a good many of them, though not by any means to all. (Not the least serious result of compulsory marriage has been the compulsory motherhood of women in whom the maternal instinct is slight — of whom there are many.) I do not mean that men should necessarily be excluded altogether from the tending of children; in many men the sense of fatherhood is very strong, in spite of the discouragement it receives under present conditions. If that discouragement were removed the paternal instinct might manifest itself in a more personal care of children; but on the whole one imagines that such personal care of children will always come more easily to woman. On the other hand, as most men are stronger muscularly than women, those departments of labour which require the exertion of considerable muscular strength must, under ordinary circumstances, naturally be monopolised by man. But between these two extremes there lies what may be called a neutral or debatable ground of labour requiring the exercise of qualities which are the exclusive property of neither sex. It is in this neutral field that the law to which I have alluded above comes into operation — the law under which the activities of women are confined to those departments of the labour market into which men do not care, or actively object, to enter. Thus, if there were no question of economic competition, it seems to me that the invasion by woman of these departments of the labour market which were formerly monopolised by men would be bound to awaken a certain amount of opposition; since her consequent desertion of the dull, unpleasant, and monotonous tasks assigned to her, might mean that these tasks would have to be performed by those who had hitherto escaped the necessity by shifting it on to her shoulders. Hence a natural and comprehensible resentment.

The average and unthinking man who passes his existence in a modern civilised town, if he were asked upon what principle the work of the world was shared between the men and the women who inhabit it, would very probably reply, in his average and unthinking way, that the idea underlying the division of labour between the sexes was the idea of sparing woman the hard bodily toil for which she was unfitted by her lack of physical strength. If that really were the principle upon which the division of labour was made, it is clear that the ordinary male clerk ought at once to change places with the ordinary housemaid or charwoman, the ordinary ticket-collector with the ordinary laundress. The physical labour of holding a pen or collecting tickets is infinitely less than the physical labour of carrying coals upstairs, scrubbing a floor, or wringing out a dirty garment. There is no particular or inevitable reason why such changes should not be made — and no further away than France housemaid's duties are very commonly performed by men. Clerking, the duties of a ticket-collector, laundry-work and housework are all situated upon that neutral ground of labour to which I have alluded above; they are forms of work which do not call for the exercise of qualities peculiar to either sex, and which, therefore, can be equally well performed by persons of either sex.

To take another instance. In most civilised countries the rougher branches of agriculture are looked upon as work which is unsuited to women, because making too heavy demands upon their strength. Amongst primitive and semi-civilised peoples, on the other hand, the tilling of the soil is often left entirely to women; while the dweller in towns — who usually has most to say about these matters — would probably be astonished if he realised how largely women's work is employed, even in Europe, in the rougher processes of agriculture. (Within less than a twenty-four hours' journey from London I have seen a woman yoked to a plough.) In certain small communities on the Breton coast I understand that the work of agriculture is carried on entirely by the women of the community; the men — fishermen by trade — occupying themselves during the long periods of enforced idleness between the fishing seasons by dressmaking for the household, and other forms of sewing. I have before me, as I write, a specimen of the needlework of one of these Breton fishermen: a penwiper, neatly cut and sewn, and quaintly ornamented with a design in yellow thread — the sort of trifle that we should regard as an essentially feminine production. To me such a division of labour does not seem in the least 'unnatural'. Having regard to the circumstances, I can well understand that the man who took needle and scissors to produce my penwiper — and who had his fill of stormy and open-air toil at other times — should prefer to set his hand to a restful occupation which would keep him in his home, rather than to the plough or the spade, which would take him out of it.

In the beginning of things, labour seems to have been divided between the sexes on a fairly simple plan. Man did most of the hunting and most of the fighting; and woman, only joining in the hunting and fighting if necessity arose, did all the rest. In savage tribes which have suddenly come under the domination of a civilised race — a domination which usually means not only the cessation of tribal warfare, but a rapid decrease in the raw material of the chase — the male, debarred from the exercise of his former avocations, frequently refuses to do anything at all. Deprived of the only work proper to man, and disinclined, at first, to undertake the work he considers proper to woman, he is apt to fold his hands and exist in idleness on what is, to all intents and purposes, the slave-labour of his female belongings. The distaste of certain South African races for what we esteem men's work is well known, and has had political consequences before now; and it is said that in some primitive American tribes a man would consider that he demeaned himself by undertaking such strictly feminine work as the hewing and carrying of wood. (One is led to the conclusion that the idea of woman as a wife-and-mother-and-nothing-else must be of comparatively modern growth. 'Natural' man did not think of her in that light at all; he had so many other uses for her. Or, perhaps, one might put it that his definition of the duties of a wife and mother was comprehensive.)

The early arts and the first processes of manufacture are supposed to have originated with that half of the human race which is now denied invention and initiative — arising naturally out of her more complicated duties and more settled habits of living. Woman was certainly, and all unknown to herself, the civilising agent in the primitive community. The hut, clearing, or cave where she tended the hearth and carried on her rude industries, and whither her man returned from his roaming expeditions, was the germ and nucleus of the city where her descendants now dwell.

It was not until the world grew more crowded, less of a place to fight in, less of a place to hunt in, that man began to consider other means and take to other ways of earning his living — to dig and to engage in manufactures. In other words, he began to invade the sphere of woman (it is as well to remember this), and to parcel out and divide the industries hitherto monopolised by her. This process of parcelling out and division was carried out in accordance with the principle already mentioned — that woman was to keep those trades which man did not care to embark upon; and, roughly speaking, his preference in the matter has always been for those callings and professions which ensured him, in addition to his livelihood, and, if possible, a prospect of advancement, a certain amount of variety in his existence, and a certain amount of intercourse with his fellows. His tendency, therefore, has been to annex those trades which afforded him the desired amount of variety, intercourse, and prospect of advancement, and to leave to woman the monotonous, prospectless, and isolated callings — callings which were usually connected with the home; and that tendency seems to have continued with very little check until the beginning of the revolution in our social and industrial system which was brought about by the introduction of machinery — a revolution which, incidentally and amongst other things, is changing almost beyond recognition the institution known as the home, modifying the relations of the sexes, and completely altering the position of woman by forcing her, whether she likes it or not, to stand on her own feet.

I have dwelt at some length upon this tendency in the dominant sex — the outcome of no deliberate selfishness, but of the natural and instinctive human impulse to take the line of least resistance and get what one wants in the easiest way — because it seems to me to afford the only reasonable explanation of the customary hard and fast division of labour between an ordinary man and an ordinary wife. Fundamentally, I can see no reason why it should be the duty of the wife, rather than of the husband, to clean doorsteps, scrub floors, and do the family cooking. Men are just as capable as women of performing all these duties. They can clean doorsteps and scrub floors just as well as women; they can cook just as well as women, sometimes better. Why, then, should it be assumed that it is the natural thing for a married woman to take over these particular departments of work, and that when a bride undertakes to love, honour, and obey her husband, she also undertakes to scrub his floors and fry his steaks? The answer to that question seems to be, not that it is natural for a woman to like a form of labour which is usually monotonous and without prospect, but that it is quite natural for a man to dislike it — and therefore leave it to some one else.

One of the best examples, in a small way, of the tendency I have been speaking of I got not long ago from a friend of mine, a woman of the working-class. I happened to be one of an audience she was addressing, when she suddenly put to it the unexpected question — 'Why does the father carve the joint in rich people's houses, when in poor people's houses it is the mother who carves it?' One, at least, of her audience was entirely at a loss for an answer to the conundrum until it was duly furnished by the speaker — running as follows: 'In rich people's houses the father carves the joint, because there is always enough to go round and the carver can help himself to the tit-bits. In poor people's houses the mother carves the joint, because there mayn't be always enough to go round and the carver gets the last helping.' I have no doubt that her explanation of the two customs is correct. Where the labour of carving is a pleasant duty, likely to bring its reward, it is performed by the head of the household; where it is an unpleasant duty, incurring penalty in the place of reward, the head of the household decides to pass it on to some one else. I do not mean that he decides it after due and selfish deliberation — he simply obeys a natural unthinking impulse.

It will be urged, of course, that motherhood and the care of children being the central point and fundamental interest in a woman's life, the domestic duties and arts spring naturally from that central point and group themselves around it; and that this, and not any question of masculine likes and dislikes in the matter, is the real reason why, all over the world, certain forms of labour, some of them of a drudging and unpleasant nature, are thrust upon her — by the decree of providence, and not by the will of her husband.

I am always suspicious of those decrees of providence which run parallel to the interests of persons who have taken it upon themselves to expound providential wisdom; and as I have already explained, I am inclined to doubt that there exists in every woman an overpowering maternal instinct which swamps all other interests and desires. But even if, for the sake of argument, the universality of an overpowering maternal instinct be admitted, it is legitimate to point out that housework and its unpaid drudgery is not only performed in the interests of children. It is performed in childless households; it is expected, as a matter of course, by fathers from their daughters, by brothers from their sisters. It is performed, in short, in the interests of the man quite as much as in the interests of the child — perhaps more, since, in a busy household, the child, so far from being the central point and pivot of an establishment, is often attended to only incidentally, and in the time that can be snatched from other duties. Further, in the numerous households where husband and wife alike go out to work — perhaps at the same form of labour, as is the case in many factory districts — the woman on returning home (after working all day, just as her husband does, to contribute her share of the weekly expenses necessary for the support of household and children) has to cook, clean, sew, etc., in the time which her husband can employ as he chooses. In such instances the wife has taken her share in what are usually considered the typical duties of a husband, and it would be only reasonable to suppose that, in the consequent rearrangement of the domestic economy, the husband, as a matter of course, would take his share in the typical duties of a wife. In some cases, no doubt, he does; but as a general rule the household duties are left to the woman, in exactly the same manner as they would be left to her if she did not leave her house to work for a wage. And they are left to her simply because her husband considers them tiresome or unpleasant, and therefore declines to perform them.

I have laid stress on the conditions under which woman's work as a wife, mother, and housekeeper is usually carried on, because it seems to me that the influence of those conditions has extended far beyond that narrow circle of the home to which, until comparatively lately, her energies have been confined. It was within the four walls of the home that man learned to look upon her as a being whose share of work was always the unpleasant share, and whose wages were the lowest wages that could possibly be given. And — which is far worse — she learned to look upon herself in the same light, as a creature from whom much must be demanded and to whom little must be given. Small wonder, then, with that age-long tradition behind her, that when she is forced out into the world, unorganised and unprepared, she finds it hard to get even a living wage for the work of her head and hands — and that when you speak of a sweated you mean a woman's trade.

There is, so far as I can see, only one way in which woman can make herself more valued, and free herself from the necessity of performing duties for which she gets neither thanks nor payment. She must do as men have always done in such a situation — shirk the duties.

Nine

There is one element in the relations between man and wife to which, as yet, I have hardly referred. I mean that element which is known as the exercise of protection by the stronger over the weaker — by the man over the woman. In considering the rewards of wifehood, great or small, it cannot, of course, be passed over without examination, since it seems to be assumed that a man pays his wife for services unpaid in other ways by defending her against perils, physical or otherwise.

Now there can be no doubt that in former ages and all over the world — as in certain regions of the world to-day — this physical protection of the weaker by the stronger, of the woman by the man, was a thing that really counted in marriage. The women of a savage tribe which was constantly at war with surrounding savage tribes would have to rely on the strength and skill in warfare of their men to deliver them from capture or death. In such a primitive state of affairs every man might be called upon at any moment to exercise in his own person duties of defence and protection which the average man now delegates to the paid soldier and the paid policeman. In the beginning of things the head of every family possessed the right of private war and private justice, and it was on his success in both these fields of activity that the lives and the welfare of his womenfolk and children would very largely depend. It was only by virtue of his strength that he could maintain possession of his property in goods or in human flesh. It was by virtue of his superior strength that he reduced woman to subjection, and in return, and as a form of payment for her toil, defended her from the attacks of others. So arose and originated the idea of the physical protection necessarily meted out by husband to wife; an idea real enough in the beginning. Circumstances alter cases; but they often take a long time to alter ideas, and this particular one continues to flourish luxuriantly in places where the order of things that gave it birth has passed into the forgotten. One still hears people talk as if a clerk or a greengrocer's assistant, married in a suburban chapel and going to Cliftonville for his honeymoon, undertook thereby to shelter his better half from Heaven knows what of vague and mysterious peril. From other times and other manners, beginning with the days when a stone axe formed a necessary part of a bride-groom's wedding garment, into places where moral force has fought the worst of its bitter battle with physical force, into days when private war is called murder and the streets are policed, there has come down the superstition that the ordinary civilised man performs doughty feats of protection for the benefit of the ordinary civilised wife. And it seems to be accepted that that element of protection is a natural and unavoidable element in the relations of married man and woman — even of married man and woman living in a suburban flat.

Once upon a time it was a natural and unavoidable element in the relations of every married couple; just as it was natural and unavoidable, once upon a time, that the unwarlike and commercially-minded burghers of a mediaeval city should bargain with a neighbouring and predatory baron to keep at bay — for a consideration — other barons no less predatory but a little less neighbouring. That sort of arrangement, I believe, was fairly common in the Middle Ages when predatory barons were in a position which enabled them to bend the law to their own liking, and when the obvious thing for honest and peaceable men to do was to set a thief to catch a thief. A recognised institution in its day, this particular form of protection passed with the growth of a central authority, with the suppression of private warfare and the substitution of a national for a tribal ideal. Instead of paying blackmail to a brigand, the city, in its later days, organised a police force of its own and contributed its share towards the upkeep of a national army. And the overlord vanished because, his duties having been taken away from him, there was nothing left for him to do. Much the same sort of thing has happened in other directions; increasing civilisation has left other than barons without the duties that formerly appertained to their position. Like the protective functions of the overlord, the protective functions of the husband have been centralised and nationalised, regulated by the community and delegated to the soldier and the policeman. Where stable government exists the number of men who offer up their lives each year in actual defence of their own hearths and their own wives is, I imagine, small, so small that I do not suppose the insurance companies take much account of it in estimating their risks. I have not the least intention of casting any reflection upon the courage of the average civilised husband or inferring that he is not willing to offer up his life in defence of his better half if called upon to do so; I merely state the obvious fact that he is not very often called upon to make the sacrifice. Even in those countries where universal military service is established, the duty of defending the national (not the individual) hearth and home falls last upon men who are married and have a family to support; it is the young, unmarried men who are called upon to form the first line of defence and defiance. And in ordinary every day life it is the strong arm of the law and not the strong arm of the individual husband which secures a woman from hurt and molestation. If it were not so the unprotected spinster would be in a truly piteous plight. As a matter of fact, she usually finds that the ordinary constable is quite adequate for all her requirements in the protective line.

Closely allied to this idea of individual masculine protection is that other, and still more vaguely nebulous, idea of chivalry or preferential treatment of women in general by men in general. Which necessitates an inquiry into what the average modern man really means when he talks of chivalry in this connection.

Frankly, it does not seem to me that he means very much. My own experience leads me to define chivalry — not the real thing, but the term as it is commonly used, say, in the public press — to define chivalry as a form, not of respect for an equal, but of condescension to an inferior; a condescension which expresses itself in certain rules of behaviour where non-essentials are involved. In very few really essential matters between man and woman is the chivalric principle allowed to get so much as a hearing; in practically all such matters it is, as I have already pointed out, an understood thing that woman gets the worst of the bargain, does the unpleasant work in the common division of labour, and, when blame is in question, sits down under the lion's share of it. In return for this attitude on her part — which, if voluntary, would be really chivalrous, but being involuntary is merely servile — man undertakes to regulate his conduct towards her by certain particular forms of outward deference. His attitude, so far as one can gather, is something like this: as long as you refrain from coming into competition with us, as long as you will allow us to look down upon you, as long as you are content to regard yourselves not only as our dependents, but as persons sent into the world to minister to our comforts and our pleasures, so long shall our outward behaviour towards you be framed in a particular code of manners which secures you preferential treatment in unimportant matters. But, in order to secure this preferential treatment in unimportant matters, you must put no strain upon our courtesy, and you must defer to our wishes in more important things; you must not trespass upon the domain that we have reserved for our own use, you must not infringe the rules which have been laid down for your guidance and whose aim is to secure our own comfort.

In other words, what is commonly known as 'chivalry' is not a spontaneous virtue or impulse on the part of modern man, but the form in which he pays his debt for value received from woman. Directly she fails to fulfil her own important share of the bargain, he considers himself at liberty to refuse payment; at least, one must conclude so from the frequency with which the 'independent' woman of to-day is threatened with the extinction of chivalry if she continued to assert herself in a manner which may be consistent with her own desires, but which is not consistent with the desires of average male humanity. Looked at in that light, the preferential code of manners, which is all that is usually understood by chivalry, bears distinct resemblance to the sugar that attempts to veil the flavour of a pill or the jam that does its best to conceal the noxiousness of a lurking powder. By a simple process of exchange and barter outward deference on the one side is given in payment for real deference and subjection on the other; and, that being the case, it is quite open to woman to look into the terms of her bargain, reconsider them, and ask herself whether she is not paying too high a price for value received. For, with every respect for courtesy, the opening of a door and the lifting of a hat, however reverential, are among the small things of life.

It will no doubt be objected that chivalry is something infinitely greater than what I have called outward forms of deference. I agree that that is not the true meaning of the word; but I maintain that, in general practice, the virtue of chivalry, in so far as it enters into the daily lives of most women, amounts to outward forms of deference and little more. As soon as we come to essentials, we realise that the counteracting principle will inevitably be brought into play — the principle that the woman must always be sacrificed to the interests of the man.

There are, of course, exceptions to that rule — and noble ones. It is written that in common danger of death the stronger must think first, not of his own life, but of the lives of those weaker and dependent upon him; and whatever other laws a man might break with impudence and impunity, he would very certainly be ashamed to confess to a breach of this particular commandment. One respects such habitual obedience as fine and finely disciplined; but it is not decrying it to point out that not every man is called upon to exercise it and that the form of chivalry cultivated by most is necessarily of a less strenuous type. And into chivalry of the less strenuous type the idea of self-sacrifice in essentials does not as a rule enter, since it is, as I have already shown, in the nature of a reward or payment for self-sacrifice in others.

I am quite aware that there are a great many women of the upper and middle classes — women, for the most part, who lead a leisured and comfortable existence — who attach an inordinately high value to outward forms of deference from the men with whom they come in contact. Considering their training and education, and the trend of their whole lives, it is perhaps only natural that they should. The aim of that training and education has been, as I have shown, not to develop their individuality and capacities, but to make themselves and their actions pleasing to the men with whom they may happen to come in contact; and, that being so, approval from the men with whom they may happen to come in contact is naturally a thing of the utmost importance to them. To lack it is to lack the whole reward of a well-spent life. By women with this narrow outlook on the world superficial courtesies and superficial deference are interpreted to mean approval and, therefore, success in pleasing — almost the only form of success open to them. Further, the lives of such women are usually sheltered, and thus they do not have very much opportunity of realising that the meed of ceremony to which they are accustomed is largely a tribute paid, not to themselves or to their womanhood, but to the particular leisured class to which they happen to belong.

Whatever the reason, it is certain that many women of the 'comfortable' class do cling desperately and rather pathetically to the idea of their little privileges in this respect; I have over and over again heard such women oppose efforts to better their own position and that of others simply on the ground that 'men would not treat us in the same way — there would be no chivalry, they would not be polite to us any longer.' Apparently the good souls are under the impression that no man is ever polite to a person he does not despise; and this sort of argument shows how completely those who use it have learned to substitute the shadow for the reality and dissociate what is commonly called chivalry from respect. To them masculine courtesy is an expression not of reverence for women, but of more or less kindly contempt for them — and they are quite content that it should be so. Personally, this attitude — an attitude of voluntary abasement assumed in order that man may know the pleasure of condescension — is the only thing that ever makes me ashamed of being a woman; since it is the outward and visible expression of an inward servility that has eaten and destroyed a soul.

Ten

Modern chivalry, then, has been narrowed down, if not in theory, at any rate in practice, to a code of deferential behaviour affecting such matters and contingencies as the opening of doors, the lifting of hats, and the handing of teacups; but not touching or affecting the pre-eminence and predominance of man in the more important interests of life. At its best, such a code of behaviour is a meritorious attempt to atone for advantage in essentials by self-abnegation in non-essentials; at its worst, it is simply an expression of condescension.

That there is a chivalry which means something other and more than this — which is based upon the idea, not of condescension, but of real respect for women — I shall not deny; but it is comparatively rare — for the simple reason that the qualities encouraged and fostered in the ordinary woman are not the sort of qualities which command respect. They may have other merits, but that one they lack. For, be it noted, respect is a tribute to be commanded; not a reward to be won by supplication, by abasement, or compliance with the wishes of others. We do not necessarily like what we respect — for instance, the strength, the skill, and the resources of an enemy; and we do not necessarily respect in other people qualities which, in our own interests, we should like them to possess — qualities of subservience, submission, and timidity, which we are quite willing to make use of even while we despise them.

This latter attitude, it seems to me, is the attitude of man to woman. For generations the training of woman has been directed towards the encouragement in her of certain qualities and characteristics — such as subservience, narrowness of mind, stupidity — all of them designed to promote the comfort and well-being of her owner, but none of them calculated to arouse in him a sensation of esteem. One may be kind to a person who is subservient, narrow-minded, and stupid; but one does not respect that person. It is no reproach whatever to a man to say that he does not respect women so long as he believes (and is encouraged to believe) that their only interests in life are the interests represented in a newspaper by the page entitled, *Woman's World,* or the *Sphere of Woman* — a page dealing with face-powder, frilled nightgowns, and anchovy toast. No sane and intelligent man could feel any respect for a woman whose world was summed up in these things. If the face-powder were applied with discretion and the directions on the subject of anchovy toast carried out with caution, he might find her an ornament as well as a convenience in his home; but it would be impossible for him to respect her, because she would not be, in the proper sense of the word, respectable. If he encourages the type, it is not because he respects it.

It may, of course, be urged that woman's claim to reverence and respect is based on far higher and surer ground than mere intelligence, or even character — on the fulfilment of her duties as wife and mother. Personally, I fail to see that any very great measure of respect or reverence is dealt out to her on this or any other ground — except, perhaps, now and again on paper; and even if it were, I should not, under present conditions, consider it justified. As long as the fulfilment of those duties is not a purely voluntary action on the part of woman, it gives her no claim upon any one's respect. Heroism under pressure is not heroism at all; and there is, to my mind, nothing the least exalted or noble in bringing up children, cooking chops, and cleaning doorsteps merely because very few other ways of earning a decent living happen to be open to you. And so long as marriage and motherhood are not matters of perfectly free choice on the part of the majority of women, so long will the performance of the duties incurred by marriage and motherhood, however onerous and however important, constitute no particular title to respect.

In so far as men do respect women, and not despise them, it seems to me that they respect them for exactly those qualities which they esteem in each other — and which, paradoxically enough, are for the most part exactly those qualities which they have done their best to erase and eradicate from the feminine character. The characteristics which make a man or a woman 'respectable' are not the characteristics of subserviency and servility; on the contrary, those particular characteristics, even when encouraged for interested reasons, are rightly and naturally regarded with contempt. They may be more comfortable to live with — man evidently thinks so — but, comfortable or not, they are despised instinctively. They have their reward, no doubt; but that reward is not reverence and respect — since reverence and respect must be commanded, not coaxed or cringed for. A woman who insists on flinging aside the traditions of her early training, standing on her own feet, fighting her own battle, and doing that which is right in her own eyes, may not get from man anything more than respect, but, in the long run, she will certainly get that. It may be given grudgingly, but it will be given, all the same; since courage and independence of thought are qualities respectable in themselves. And, on the other hand, and however much he may desire to do so, it is, I should say, quite impossible for any thinking man to entertain a real reverence and esteem for a section of humanity which he believes to exist solely in order to perform certain animal functions connected with, and necessary to, the reproduction of the race. After all, it is not upon the performance of a purely animal function that a human being should found his or her title to respect; if woman is reverenced only because she reproduces her kind, a still higher meed of reverence is due to the rabbit.

And in this connection it is interesting to note that the mediaeval institution of chivalry, with its exalted, if narrow, ideal of reverence for, and service of, womanhood, took its rise and flourished in times when the housekeeping and child-bearing trade was not the only occupation open to women; when, on the contrary, they had, in the religious life, an alternative career, equally honoured with, if not more honoured than, marriage; and when it was not considered essential to the happiness and well-being of every individual woman to pair off, after the fashion of the animals going into the ark. Whatever the defects and drawbacks of conventual life, it stood for the principle, denied before and since, that woman had an existence of her own apart from man, a soul to be saved apart from man. It was a flat defiance of the theory that she came into the world only to marry and reproduce her kind; it acknowledged and admitted the importance of her individual life and conduct; in short, it recognised her as something besides a wife and a mother, and gave her other claims to respect than that capacity for reproduction which she shared with the lower animals. Further, by making celibacy an honourable instead of a despised estate, it must have achieved an important result from an economic point of view; it must have lessened the congestion in the marriage market by lessening the number of women who regarded spinsterhood as the last word in failure. It enhanced the value of the wife and mother by making it not only possible, but easy, for her to become something else. It opened up a career to an ambitious woman; since, in the heyday of the Church, the head of a great community of nuns was something more than a recluse — a power in the land, an administrator of estates. None of these things, of course, were in the minds of those who instituted the celibate, conventual life as a refuge from the world; they were its unforeseen results, but none the less real because unforeseen. They followed on the institution of the conventual life for woman because it represented the only organised attempt ever made to free her from the necessity of compulsory marriage and child-bearing.

I have no bias, religious or otherwise, in favour of the conventual life, which, as hitherto practised, is no doubt open to objection on many grounds; but it seems to me that any institution or system which admits or implies a reason for woman's existence other than sexual intercourse and the reproduction of her kind must tend inevitably to raise the position not only of the celibate woman, but, indirectly, of the wife and mother. In its palmy days, when it was a factor not only in the spiritual life of a religious body, but in the temporal life of the State, the convent, with all its defects, must have stood for the advancement of women; and if it had never come into existence, I very much doubt whether the injunctions laid upon knighthood would have included respect for and service of womanhood.

The upheaval which we term the Reformation, whatever its other merits, was distinctly anti-feminist in its tendencies. Where it did not sweep the convent away altogether, it narrowed its scope and sapped its influence; and, being anti-feminist, evolved no new system to take the place of that which it had swept away. The necessity of replacing the monk by the schoolmaster was recognised, but not the necessity of replacing the nun by the schoolmistress; the purely physical and reproductive idea of woman being once again uppermost, the need for training her mind no longer existed. The masterful women of the Renaissance had few successors; and John Knox, with his *Monstrous Regiment of Women*, was but the mouthpiece of an age which was setting vigorously to work to discourage individuality and originality in the weaker sex by condemning deviations from the common type to be burnt as witches.

This favourite pastime of witch-burning has not, I think, been sufficiently taken into account in estimating the reason for the low standard of intelligence attained by women at a time when men were making considerable progress in social and intellectual fields. The general impression appears to be that only old, ugly, and decrepit hags fell victims to popular superstition or the ingenuity of the witch-finder; but, as a matter of fact, when the craze for witch-finding was at its height, any sort of peculiarity, even beauty of an unusual and arresting type, seems to have been sufficient to expose a woman to the suspicion of secret dealings with the Prince of Darkness. At first sight it seems curious (since the religious element in a people is usually the feminine element) that the Prince of Darkness should have confined his dealings almost exclusively to women — it has been estimated that wizards were done to death in the proportion of one to several thousand witches; but on further consideration one inclines to the belief that the fury of witch-burning by which our ancestors were possessed must have been prompted by motives other than purely devotional. In all probability those motives were largely unconscious; but the rage of persecution against the witch has so much in common with the customary masculine policy of repressing, at any cost, all deviations from the type of wife-and-mother-and-nothing-else, that one cannot help the suspicion that it was more or less unconsciously inspired by that policy.

Eleven

So far I have treated of the various influences which have been brought to bear upon women with the object of fitting them for the trade to which the male half of humanity desired to confine them; and I have, I hope, made it clear that, to a certain extent, these influences have defeated their own ends by discouraging the intelligence which ought to be a necessary qualification for motherhood, even if it is not a necessary qualification for wifehood. It remains to be considered what effect this peculiar training for one particular and peculiar trade has had upon woman's activity in those departments of the world's work which are not connected with marriage and motherhood, how it has acted upon her capacity for wage-earning and breadwinning on her own account, how it has affected her power of achievement in every other direction; what, in short, has been its effect upon woman in the life that she leads apart from man. (I must ask the male reader to be good enough to assume, even if he cannot honestly believe, that woman can, and occasionally does, lead a life apart from man.)

And one notes, to begin with, that the customary training, or lack of training, for marriage tends almost inevitably to induce that habit and attitude of mind which is known as amateurishness. And particularly, I should say, in the large class of society, which we describe roughly as the middle class; where the uncertainty with regard to the position, profession and consequent manner of living of the probable husband is so great as to make a thorough and businesslike training for the future nearly an impossibility. The element of chance — an element which plays such a very large part in the life, at any rate, of the average married woman — may upset all calculations based on the probable occupation and requirements of the husband, render carefully acquired accomplishments useless or unnecessary, and call for the acquirement of others hitherto unwanted and even undreamed of. Two sisters brought up in exactly the same surroundings and educated in exactly the same manner may marry, the one a flourishing professional or city man, who expects her to dress well, talk well, give good dinners and generally entertain his friends; the other a man whose work lies on the frontier of civilisation where she will find it necessary to learn something of the management of horses and to manufacture her own soap and candles. While a third sister in the same family may never marry at all, but pass her life in furnished apartments, being waited on by landladies. These may be extreme, but they are not very unusual instances of the large part taken by sheer chance in the direction of a woman's life and the consequent impossibility of mapping out and preparing for the future. Hence a lack of thoroughness and an attitude towards life of helplessness and what I have called amateurishness. (The corresponding male attitude is found in the unskilled labourer of the 'odd job' type.) Hence also the common feminine habit of neglecting more solid attainments in order to concentrate the energies on an endeavour to be outwardly attractive.

This concentration of energy on personal adornment, usually attributed to vanity or overflowing sexuality, is, so far as I can see, largely the outcome of a sound business instinct. For, be it remembered, that the one solid fact upon which an ordinary marriageable girl has to build the edifice of her life is the fact that men are sensitive to, and swayed by, that quality in woman which is called personal charm. What else her future husband will demand of her is more or less guess-work — nothing upon which to raise a solid foundation of preparation for his requirements and her own. He may require her to sit at the head of his table and talk fashionable gossip to his friends; he may require her to saddle horses and boil soap; the only thing she can be fairly certain of is that he will require her to fulfil his idea of personal attractiveness. As a matter of business then, and not purely from vanity, she specialises in personal attractiveness; and the care, the time and the thoroughness which many women devote to their own adornment, the choosing of their dresses and the curling of their hair is thoroughly professional and a complete contrast to their amateurishness in other respects.

The cultivation of personal charm, sometimes to the neglect of more solid and valuable attainments, is the more natural, because, as I have already pointed out, the material rewards of wifehood and motherhood have no connection at all with excellence in the performance of the duties of wifehood and motherhood — the wage paid to a married woman being merely a wage for the possession of her person. That being the case, the one branch of woman's work which is likely to bring her a material reward in the shape of an economically desirable husband is cultivation of a pleasing exterior and attractive manners; and to this branch of work she usually, when bent on marriage, applies herself in the proper professional spirit. A sensible, middle-class mother may insist on her daughter receiving adequate instruction in the drudgery of household work and cookery; but if the daughter should be fortunate enough to marry well such instruction will be practically wasted, since the scrubbing, the stewing, the frying and the making of beds will inevitably be deputed to others. And the sensible, middle-class mother is quite aware that her daughter's chance of marrying well and shirking disagreeable duties does not depend on the excellent manner in which she performs those duties, but on the quality of her personal attractions. The cultivation of her personal attractions, therefore, is really a more important and serious business for the girl who desires to marry than the acquirement of domestic accomplishments, which may, or may not, be useful in her after life, and which in themselves are unlikely to secure her the needful husband. This state of things is frankly recognised in the upper or wealthier ranks of society. There the typical domestic arts find practically no place in a girl's scheme of training which is directed solely towards the end of making her personally attractive and therefore desirable. Which means, of course, that those women who are in a position to do so concentrate their energies on the cultivation of those particular outward qualities by which alone they can hope to satisfy their ambition, their need for comfort, luxury, etc., or their desire to bring children into the world. They recognise that however much man may profess to admire the domestic and maternal qualities in woman, it is not that side of her which arouses in him the desire for possession, and that the most effective means of arousing that desire for possession is personal charm. We have been told that every woman is at heart a rake; it would, I think, be more correct to say that every woman who desires to attract some member of the opposite sex so that she may marry and bear children must, whatever she is at heart, be something of a rake on the surface.

With girls of the working-class, of course, a certain amount of training in domestic work is usually gone through, since it is obvious that domestic work will be required of them in after life; but even in the humblest ranks of society the rule holds good that it is personal attractiveness and not skill in the duties required of a wife and mother which makes a girl sought after and admired by the opposite sex. Consequently even working-class wives and mothers, women who have no chance of deputing their duties to paid servants, are frequently nothing but amateurs at their trade — which they have only acquired incidentally. In practically all ranks of society the real expert in housekeeping or in the care and management of infants is the 'unattached' woman who works in other people's houses and attends to other people's children. She is the professional who knows her business and earns her living by it; the wife and mother, as often as not, being merely the amateur.

Human nature, and especially male human nature, being what it is, I do not know whether it is possible or even desirable that this state of things should be altered. My object in calling attention to it is not to suggest alteration (I have none to suggest), but simply to point out that women who are brought up in the expectation of marriage and nothing but marriage are almost of necessity imbued with that spirit of amateurishness which makes for inefficiency; and that this spirit has to be taken into account in estimating their difficulties where they have to turn their attention to other trades than marriage.

There are several other respects in which the marriage tradition (by which I mean the practical identification during many generations of womanhood with wifehood and motherhood) acts as a drag and a hindrance to the woman who, married or unmarried and with or against her will, has been swept out of the sacred and narrow sphere of home to compete for a wage in the open market.

(Be it remembered that she is now numbered not by hundreds or thousands, but by millions.) As I have already pointed out, the trade of marriage is, by its very nature, an isolated trade, permitting of practically no organisation or common action amongst the workers; and consequently the marriage-trained woman (and nearly all women are marriage trained — or perhaps it would be more correct to say marriage expectant) enters industrial or commercial life with no tradition of such organisation and common action behind her.

I do not think that the average man realises how much the average woman is handicapped by the lack of this tradition, nor does he usually trouble to investigate the causes of his own undoubted superiority in the matter of combination and all that combination implies. In accordance with his usual custom of explaining the shortcomings of womanhood by an inferiority that is inherent and not artificial and induced, he assumes that women cannot combine for industrial and other purposes because it is 'natural' for them to be jealous and distrustful of one another. (This assumption is, of course, an indirect compliment to himself, since the jealousy and distrust of women for each other is understood to be inspired solely by their overpowering desire to attract the admiration of the opposite sex.)

This simple and — to man — flattering explanation of woman's inferiority in this respect completely fails to take into account the fact that the art of combination for a common purpose has been induced in one half of humanity by influences which have not been brought to bear upon the other half. I do not suppose that even the firmest and most hardened believer in woman's essential disloyalty, treachery and incapacity for common action, would venture to maintain that if all the men of past generations had been compelled to earn their living at isolated forms of labour — say, as lighthouse-keepers or shepherds in mountainous districts — the faculty of united action for common ends would be very highly developed amongst them. As I have already tried to show, in the division of labour between the two sexes man has almost invariably reserved for himself (having the power to do so, and because he considered them preferable) those particular occupations which brought him into frequent contact with his fellows, which entailed meeting others and working side by side with them; and this frequent contact with his fellows was, in itself, a form of education which has been largely denied to the other half of humanity. Woman's intercourse with her kind has been much more limited in extent, and very often purely and narrowly social in character. Until comparatively recent years it was unusual for women to form one of a large body of persons working under similar conditions and conscious of similar interests. It is scarcely to be wondered at that the modern system of industrialism with its imperative need for co-operation and common effort should have found her — thanks to her training — unprepared and entirely at a disadvantage.

It must be remembered also that the generality and mass of women have never come under the direct influence of two of the most potent factors in the social education and evolution of man as we know him — war and politics. However decivilising an agency war may appear to-day, it has not been without its civilising influence, since it was through the necessity of standing side by side for purposes of offence and defence that man first learned the art of combining for a common end, and acquired the virtues, at first purely military, that, in course of time and under different circumstances, were to develop into civic virtues. The camp was the state in embryo, the soldier the citizen in embryo, and the military tradition the collective and social tradition of organisation for a common purpose and common interests. In the face of a common peril, such as war, men readily forget their differences and work shoulder to shoulder. Hence an appeal to the fears or the warlike spirit of a discontented people is the instinctive refuge of a government in difficulties, since there is no means so effective for producing at least a passing phase of unity amongst the jarring elements of a nation.

Woman, so far as one can judge, is, when occasion arises, just as much influenced by that necessity of common action in a common danger which first produced unity of effort and public spirit in man; but for her, as a rule, occasion has not arisen. Now and again under exceptional circumstances, such as a desperate and hard-fought siege, she has shown that the sense of peril acts upon her in exactly the same way as it acts upon her brethren; but the actual waging of battle has not often, even in the most turbulent of ages, entered into her life to teach her (along with other and less desirable lessons) the lesson of united effort and subordination of individual interest to the common weal.

The exclusion of woman from the arena of politics has barred to her another method of acquiring the art of combination and the strength that inevitably springs from it; an exclusion based upon the deep-rooted masculine conviction that she exists not for her own benefit and advantage, but for the comfort and convenience of man. Granted that she came into the world for that purpose only, the right of effective combination in her own interests is clearly unnecessary and undesirable, since it might possibly lead to results not altogether conducive to the comfort and convenience of man. The masculine attitude in this matter seems quite logical.

Twelve

The above are not the only respects in which the peculiar training for, or expectation of, marriage acts disadvantageously upon woman as soon as she steps outside the walls of the home to earn her bread by other means than household work and the bearing and rearing of children. I have already pointed out that the wage she receives for her work as a wife and mother is the lowest that she can receive — a wage of subsistence only; and I believe that the exceedingly low rate at which her services inside the home are valued has had a great deal to do with the exceedingly low value placed upon her services outside the home. Because her work as a wife and mother was rewarded only by a wage of subsistence, it was assumed that no other form of work she undertook was worthy of a higher reward; because the only trade that was at one time open to her was paid at the lowest possible rate, it was assumed that in every other trade into which she gradually forced her way she must also be paid at the lowest possible rate. The custom of considering her work as worthless (from an economic point of view) originated in the home, but it has followed her out into the world. Since the important painful and laborious toil incurred by marriage and motherhood was not deemed worthy of any but the lowest possible wage, it was only natural that other duties, often far less toilsome and important, should also be deemed unworthy of anything much in the way of remuneration.

It is very commonly assumed, of course, that the far higher rate of wage paid to a man is based on the idea that he has, or probably will have, a wife and children for whom he is bound to make provision. If this were really the case, a widow left with a young family to support by her labour, or even the mother of an illegitimate child, would be paid for her work on the same basis as a man is paid for performing similar duties. It is hardly needful to state that the mother of fatherless children is not, as a rule, paid more highly than her unmarried sister. Nor is the theory that the 'unattached' woman has only herself to support, and does not contribute to the needs of others, borne out by facts. I believe that in all ranks of society there is a pronounced disposition on the part of the family to regard the income, earned or unearned, of its female members as something in the nature of common property − the income, earned or unearned, of its male members as much more of an individual possession. Wives who work for a wage in factories, workshops, etc., usually devote the whole of their earnings to the upkeep of the home; their husbands very commonly only a part. Where sons and daughters of the same family go out to work and live under one roof, it is customary for the girls to put practically the entire amount of their wage into the common domestic fund, while their brothers, from quite early years, pay a fixed sum to cover the expenses of their board and lodging, retaining, as a matter of course, the rest of their earnings for their own individual use. And, so far as my observation goes, the same rule holds good in the upper and middle classes. In the case of any monetary difficulty, any need of financial help, the appeal, in the first instance, is nearly always made to those women of the family who are understood to be in a position to respond to it; it is tacitly assumed that they must be the first to suffer and sacrifice themselves, the men of the family being appealed to only when the women are unable or unwilling to meet the demand. My experience may be unusual, but I have met very few working-women of any class, who, earning a decent livelihood at their trade or profession, were not called upon to share their livelihood with others.

It is not, therefore, on the ground that she has no one but herself to support that a woman is almost invariably paid at a rate far lower than the wage which would be given to a man for the performance of the same work. A good many causes have combined to bring about the sweating of women customary in most, if not all, departments of the labour market; but it seems to me that not the least of those causes is the long-established usage of regarding the work of a wife in the home as valueless from the economic point of view — a thing to be paid for (if paid for at all) by occasional gushes of sentiment. Woman and wife being, according to masculine ideas, interchangeable terms, it follows that, since the labour of a wife is valueless from the economic point of view, the labour of any woman is valueless. Naturally enough, this persistent undervaluing of her services has had its effect upon woman herself; having been taught for generations that she must expect nothing but the lowest possible wage for her work, she finds considerable difficulty in realising that it is worth more — and undersells her male competitor. Thereupon angry objections on the part of the male competitor, who fails to realise that cheap female labour is one of the inevitable results of the complete acceptance by woman of the tradition of her own inferiority to himself.

One wonders what sort of generation of women that would be which grew from childhood to maturity unhampered and unhindered by the tradition of its own essential inferiority to the male half of humanity. Such a generation, at present, is a matter of pure guess-work; at least, I have never yet known the woman, however independent, self-reliant, indulged, or admired, who was not in some way affected by that tradition — consciously or unconsciously. Even those of us who have never known what it was to have a man to lean on, who have had to fight our way through the world as the average male fights his, and (since things are made infinitely easier for him) under disadvantages unknown to the average man — even we find ourselves unaccountably and at unexpected moments, acting in accordance with the belief in which we were reared, and deferring to the established tradition of inherent masculine superiority; deferring to it after a fashion that, being realised, is amusing to ourselves.

The effect of this attitude of the two sexes towards each other — an attitude of inherent and essential superiority on the one side, of inherent and essential inferiority on the other — is nearly always apparent when men and women work together at the same trade. (Apparent, at least, to the women; the men, one concludes, do not really grasp the system by which they benefit.) What I refer to is the ordered, tacit, but usually quite conscious endeavour on the part of women who work side by side with men to defer to a superiority, real or supposed, on the part of their male colleagues. Thus a woman will not only decline to call attention to a blunder or oversight on the part of a male fellow-worker, but she will, if possible, cover up his mistake, even if she suffer by it, and, at any rate, will try to give him the impression that it has escaped her notice; and this under circumstances where no sort of injury to the blunderer would be involved, and which would not prevent her from calling prompt attention to a similar slip if made by a colleague of her own sex.

I have not the slightest doubt that this tendency on the part of the working or business woman to pass over in silence the errors or mistakes of the working or business man is attributed by the latter (if, indeed, he notices it at all) to some mysterious operation of the sexual instinct; while the lack of a similar palliative attitude towards the errors and mistakes of a comrade of her own sex is, I should imagine, attributed to the natural, inevitable, and incorrigible 'cattiness' of one woman towards another — the belief in such a natural, inevitable, and incorrigible 'cattiness' being a comfortable article of the masculine faith.

The practice, it seems to me, can be explained without having recourse to the all-pervading sexual instinct (usually understood to regulate every action performed by women, from the buttoning of boots to the swallowing of cough drops). A similar practice, which can hardly have originated in the sexual instinct, obtains amongst male persons conscious of inferiority and desirous of standing well with their superiors. Junior clerks are in the habit of preserving a discreet silence with regard to errors of judgment traceable to employers, managers, and heads of firms; and the understrapper who wishes to get on in the world seldom makes a point of calling public attention to the shortcomings of foremen and others who are set in authority over him. On the contrary, he is usually — and wisely — tender towards their failings; and in the same way women are frequently tender towards the failings of those who, by virtue of sex and not of position, they believe to be set in authority over them. The attitude in this respect of working-woman to working-man is, as often as not, the attitude of a subordinate, and in itself an acknowledgment of inferiority; it has about it that tinge of servility which enjoins the turning of a blind eye to the faults of a superior.

I do not mean that the practice of condoning masculine slips is always prompted by an unthinking and servile compliance; on the contrary, it is very general amongst the increasing class of women who have learned to consider themselves as good as their masters — no less general, I should say, than amongst those who accept feminine inferiority to the male as a decree of nature. In their case the tenderness shown to masculine failings, the desire to save the masculine 'face', is usually quite conscious — I myself have heard it frankly discussed, analysed, and commented upon, time after time, by women whose occupations brought them into daily contact with men. And as the result of such frank discussion, analysis, and comment, I am inclined to believe that on the whole the motives which, in this particular class of women, induce extra consideration for the failings of a male fellow-worker are motives which, in man himself, would probably be described as chivalrous. Those of us who rub shoulders day after day with the ordinary man are perfectly well aware that the ordinary man (however much and however kindly he may seek to conceal the fact from us) regards us as his inferiors in mental capacity; and that hence he feels a peculiar and not unnatural soreness at having his errors and failings either exposed to us or exposed by us. To be shown up before your inferior brings with it, to most people, a sense of degradation; to be shown up by your inferior makes the sense of degradation yet more keenly unpleasant.

Most women who have had to pit their brain against the brain of the ordinary man have learned to realise — sometimes with amusement, sometimes, perhaps, with a measure of exultation — that the ordinary man's very belief in their essential inferiority has placed in their hands a weapon whose edge is infinitely keener than any that he possesses to use against them. It is just because she is regarded as his inferior that it is in the power of a woman to humiliate a man by the simple process of getting the better of him or holding his weaknesses up to contempt. When we quarrel or argue with an average man we know perfectly well that the vantage of the ground is ours; we know perfectly well that defeat, for us, will not bring humiliation in its train; that our antagonist, imbued with the conviction of his own intense and inherent natural superiority, will take his victory as a matter of course, and think it no disgrace to us that we have been routed by a higher intelligence than our own. We have not much to lose by defeat, we are not degraded by it — because we are the weaker side. With a man who gets the worst of it in a contest with a woman the case is quite different; since he suffers, in addition to actual defeat, all the humiliation of the stronger when beaten by the weaker, of the superior routed by the inferior force. With him defeat is not only defeat, but ignominy; his vanity is wounded and his prestige lowered. That being the case, the often expressed dislike of the clever woman — that is to say, of the woman who possesses the power to humiliate — is comprehensible enough.

It is, I think, because so many women realise how bitterly the ordinary man resents and suffers under defeat by an inferior that they humour and are tolerant of his somewhat galling attitude of what has been called — I think by Mr Bernard Shaw — intellectual condescension. They realise that the punishment which it is in their power to inflict on the offender would be out of all proportion to the unintentional offence — infinitely harder and sharper than it deserves. It is for this reason, I believe, that a woman, unless she is really stirred to strong indignation and consequent loss of self-control, will seldom attempt to 'show up' a man or drive him into a corner with unanswerable argument. Under far less provocation she would probably 'show up' or corner a woman; not because she bears a natural grudge against her own sex, but because her victory over one of her own sex is a victory over an equal, and does not necessarily involve wounded self-esteem and humiliation on the part of the vanquished. The same decent instinct which prevents a man from striking her with his clenched fist prevents her from striking too hard at his self-esteem.

As far as my experience goes, this need of humouring the belief of the average man in his own essential intellectual superiority is — though not without its amusing side — a constant source of worry and petty hindrance to the woman who has to earn her living by any form of brain-work which brings her into contact with men. It means, of course, that she puts a drag on her natural capacities, and attempts to appear less efficient than she really is; it means that ideas which one man would reveal frankly to another, suggestions which one man would make openly to another, have by her to be wrapped up, hinted at, and brought into operation by devious ways — lest the 'predominant partner' should take alarm at the possibility of being guided and prompted by an inferior intelligence. The only remedy for such a tiresome and unnecessary state of things seems to be the recognition by the 'predominant partner' of the fact that the human female is not entirely composed of sex (inferior to his own); that the brain is not a sexual organ; and that there is a neutral ground of intelligence (from which sex and its considerations are excluded) where man and woman can meet and hold intercourse, mutually unhampered by etiquette and respect for a vulnerable masculine dignity.

Thirteen

In dealing with the training for marriage, I pointed out that the qualities which make for success in the matrimonial market have little or no connection with the qualities required for the efficient performance of what is supposed to be the lifework of woman — the care of home, of husband and of children. I pointed out that the characteristics which are likely to obtain for a girl a desirable husband are not the same characteristics which will have to be brought into play if the husband, when he is obtained, is to find in her a desirable wife from the domestic point of view; and that, as a general rule, she is promoted to what should be the important and responsible position of wife and mother on the strength of attainments which have nothing to do with her fitness for the duties of that position.

The habit of judging a woman entirely by externals — appearance, dress, and manners — is not confined to the man who is in search of a wife. ('Judging' is, perhaps, the wrong phrase to use — it is, rather, a habit of resigning judgment so as to fall completely under the influence of externals.) It is very general amongst all classes of male employers, and its result is, it seems to me, a serious bar to efficiency in women's work. It pays better in the marriage market to be attractive than to be efficient, and in a somewhat lesser degree the same rule holds good in certain other departments of women's labour.

To a certain degree, of course, a man's fitness for any particular work is judged by externals; but never to the same degree as a woman's. Further, the judgment passed upon a man who is chosen to fill a vacancy because his prospective employer 'likes the look of him' has some relation to the qualities which will be required of him in the execution of the duties he will be called upon to perform — it is not biassed by irrelevant considerations of sex. A merchant will like the looks of a clerk who has the outward appearance of being smart, well mannered, well educated, and intelligent; an employer who wishes to engage a man for work which involves the carrying of heavy sacks will like the looks of a man who is possessed of muscular arms and a pair of broad shoulders. In each case he is favourably influenced by the man's externals because they seem to him to indicate the qualities which he requires in his prospective employee.

The number of men who could engage a young woman to work under them on this purely commercial and unemotional basis is, I should say, comparatively limited. I do not mean, of course, that the element of sexual attraction enters consciously into the calculations of the ordinary male employer when engaging a woman, but it certainly enters unconsciously into the calculations of a good many. A man who says that he likes the looks of a girl whom he has engaged to fill the position of typist or cashier, does not usually mean at all the same thing that he means when he says that he likes the looks of his new porter or junior clerk: he does not mean that the girl strikes him as appearing particularly fitted for the duties of typist or cashier — more alert, more intelligent, or more experienced than her unsuccessful competitors for the post — but that she has the precise shape of nose, the exact shade of hair, or the particular variety of smile or manner that he admires and finds pleasing. That is to say, he is influenced in engaging her by considerations unconnected with her probable fitness for the duties of her post, since a straight nose, auburn hair, or an engaging smile have no necessary connection with proficiency in typewriting or accounts.

I am not insisting on this intrusion of the sexual element into the business relations of men and women in any fault-finding spirit; I call attention to it merely in order to show that the conditions under which women obtain their bread in the labour market are not precisely the same as the conditions under which men obtain theirs. The intrusion of the sexual element into commercial relations may be not only unavoidable, but defensible and desirable, on other than commercial grounds; but it must be admitted that it does not tend to encourage efficiency, and the necessary discouragement of efficiency should be taken into account in estimating the value of woman's work in many departments of the labour market. I do not know whether the consciousness that they are liable to be promoted or degraded in business matters for reasons which have nothing to do with their business merits or demerits is humiliating or the reverse to the majority of women, but I do know that it is humiliating to some. (Not only to those who are deficient in good looks; I have frequently heard it resented by those whom the system favoured.) There is, too, a certain amount of irritating uncertainty about the working of the system, one man's taste in feminine looks varying from that of his next-door neighbour.

As in marriage, so in other departments of the labour market, the result of this tendency to appraise a woman on the strength of externals alone has been the intellectual deterioration of the good-looking girl. I should be very sorry to have to maintain that the good-looking girl is necessarily born less intelligent than her plainer sister; but I do not think that it can be denied that it is made extremely easy for her to become so. The conspicuously attractive girl who enters a trade or business usually takes a very short time to find out that her advancement depends more on her conspicuous personal attractions than on the steady work and strict attendance to business which has to be rendered by the woman less bountifully endowed by nature. Hence she has every inducement to be less thorough in her work, less intelligent, less reliable, and less trustworthy. The deep-rooted masculine conviction that brains and repulsiveness invariably go together in woman has this much justification in fact — the unattractive girl has to rely on her work and intelligence for advancement and livelihood, and, therefore, is not exposed to the temptation to allow her brains to run to seed as unnecessary. There is plenty of proof that the temptation is often resisted by the woman born beautiful; but she is exposed to it all the same, and is not to be over blamed when she succumbs.

There is one other disadvantage under which women's work in the paid labour market is apt to suffer — a disadvantage from which men's work is exempt, and which is directly traceable to the idea that marriage is woman's only trade. I alluded to it in an earlier chapter when I spoke of the common masculine attitude on the subject of feminine competition and the common masculine conviction that woman can somehow manage to exist without the means of supporting existence. One result of the assumption that every woman is provided with the necessaries of life by a husband, father, or other male relative is that the atmosphere which surrounds the working woman is considerably more chilling than that which surrounds the working man. His right to work is recognised; hers is not. He is more or less helped, stimulated, and encouraged to work; she is not. On the contrary, her entry into the paid labour market is often discouraged and resented. The difference is, perhaps, most clearly marked in those middle-class families where sons and daughters alike have no expectation of independence by inheritance, but where money, time, and energy are spent in the anxious endeavour to train and find suitable openings for the sons, and the daughters left to shift for themselves and find openings as they can. The young man begins his life in an atmosphere of encouragement and help; the young woman in one of discouragement, or, at best, of indifference. Her brother's work is recognised as something essentially important; hers despised as something essentially unimportant — even although it brings her in her bread. Efforts are made to stimulate his energy, his desire to succeed; no such efforts are made to stimulate hers . . . . And it is something, in starting work, to feel that you are engaged on work that matters.

Fourteen

There is one field for the activities of women upon which as yet I have not touched. It is a field where they come into direct competition with the activities of men; from which, moreover, they have not always been so completely and so jealously excluded as they have been from other spheres of the world's work. I mean the field of art and literature.

Let it be admitted, at once and without hesitation, that women have not made much of a mark in art and literature; that whatever we may achieve in the future we have given little of achievement to the past. Women artists of the first rank in whatever medium — in words, in music, in colour, in form — there have been none; and of the second rank and of the third rank but few — a very few. Let it be admitted that there has come down to us a goodly heritage of the wisdom, the aspiration and inspiration of our fathers, and that of the widsom, the aspiration and the inspiration of our mothers (for some they must have had) there has come down to us practically nothing. Art, as we know it, is a masculine product, wrought by the hands and conceived by the brains of men; the works of art that have forced themselves into the enduring life of the world have been shaped, written, builded, painted by men. They have achieved and we have imitated — on the whole, pitifully. Let that be admitted; and then let it also be admitted that it could hardly have been otherwise, and that the wonder is that woman has wrought in art not so little, but so much.

For when one comes to consider the conditions under which successive generations of women have lived such narrow life as was permitted to them, have realised such narrow ambitions as they were permitted to entertain, one begins to understand that it would have been something of a miracle if there had arisen amongst them thinkers and artists worthy to walk with the giants who have left their impress on the race. One begins to understand that it would be difficult to devise a better means of crushing out of the human system the individuality, the sincerity and the freedom of thought and expression, which is the very breath and inspiration of art, than the age-long training of woman for compulsory marriage and the compulsory duties thereof. For the qualities man has hitherto demanded and obtained in the woman he delights to honour (and incidentally to subdue) have been qualities incompatible with success in, or even with understanding of, art.

It is better, perhaps, to pause here and explain; since one is always liable to misinterpretation, and in the minds of many the term 'artist' is synonymous with a person having a tendency towards what is called free love. Let me explain, then, that by marriage, in this connection, I mean not only the estate of matrimony, but its unlegalised equivalent. As far as art is concerned, the deadening influences brought to bear upon the mistress are practically the same as those brought to bear upon the wife. (Both, for instance, are required to be attractive rather than sincere.) It is not, of course, actual sexual intercourse, legalised or the reverse, which renders a woman incapable of great creative art; it is the servile attitude of mind and soul induced in her by the influences brought to bear on her in order to fit her for the compulsory trade of marriage or its unsanctified equivalent.

In earlier chapters I have dealt with these influences at considerable length, striven to show exactly what they are and pointed out that their aim was to induce the girl who would eventually become a woman to conform to one particular and uniform type — the type admired and sought after by the largest number of men. Hence the crushing out of individuality, the elimination of the characteristics that make for variety and the development of the imitative at the expense of the creative qualities. From generation to generation the imperative necessity of earning her livelihood in the only trade that was not barred to her — of making for herself a place in the world not by the grace of God but by the favour of man — has been a ceaseless and unrelenting factor in the process of weeding out the artistic products of woman's nature. The deliberate stunting and repression of her intellectual faculties, the setting up for her admiration and imitation of the ideal of the 'silly angel', have all contributed to make of her not only a domestic animal, more or less sleek and ornamental, but a Philistine as well. Silly angels may, from the male point of view, be desirable and even adorable creatures; but one would not entrust them with the building of temples or the writing of great books. (Personally, I would not entrust them with the bringing up of children; but that is another matter.)

Art that is vital demands freedom of thought and expression, wide liberty of outlook and unhampered liberty of communication. And what freedom of thought and expression can be expected from a section of humanity which has not even a moral standard of its own, and adds to every 'thou shalt not' in its law the saving and unspoken clause, 'unless my master shall desire it of me'. A man's body may be enslaved and subdued and the faculties of the thinker and the artist still be left alive in him; but they have never been known to survive when once his mind has been subdued and brought down to utter subjection. Epictetus came of a race that had known freedom; and the nameless man who, by the waters of Babylon, poured out his passion in a torrent of hatred and desire, wore no chains on his soul when he remembered Zion.

It is the systematic concentration of woman's energies upon the acquirement of the particular qualities which are to procure her a means of livelihood by procuring her the favour of man that has deprived her, steadily and systematically, of the power of creation and artistic achievement; so much so that the commonly accepted ideals of what is known as a womanly woman are about as compatible with the ideals of an artist as oil is compatible with water. The methods of the one are repressive of self-development, calculated to ingratiate, bound by convention, servile; the methods of the other are self-assertive, experimental and untrammelled. The perfected type of wife-and-mother-and-nothing-else sees life only through another's eyes; the artist through his own. Of a system designed to foster and encourage the creative instinct in human beings one might safely predict that it would have to be the exact opposite of the system still in force for the conversion of the natural woman into the conventional wife and mother.

For the first and fundamental quality which such a system would aim at cultivating would be sincerity; which is not in itself art, but the foundation whereon art is laid. Without it, greatness in art or literature is impossible; and for this reason greatness in art or literature has hitherto been impossible to woman. The tendency and purpose of her whole training has been the repression of individuality and the inducement of artificiality; and even in the comparatively few instances where she recognises what her training has done for her, when she realises the poor thing it has made of her, and sets to work, deliberately and of firm resolve, to counteract its effects upon her life and character, it may take her the best part of a lifetime to struggle free of her chains. She does not know what she really needs, since from childhood upwards the natural bent of her inclinations has been twisted and thwarted; her only guide is what she has been told she ought to need. And thus she may waste years in attempting to draw inspiration from a form of love which it is not in her to feel, or from a passion for maternity which has no power to stir her to achievement.

This, at least, can safely be said: that any woman who has attained to even a small measure of success in literature or art has done so by discarding, consciously or unconsciously, the traditions in which she was reared, by turning her back upon the conventional ideals of dependence that were held up for her admiration in her youth.

Fifteen

In dealing with this problem of the inferior place hitherto occupied by woman in literature and art, let me admit, frankly and at once, that I have none of the qualifications of a critic. Of the technique of any branch of creative art I know practically nothing; nor can I say that I have any great measure of curiosity concerning it. I must confess to being one of that large mass of unenlightened persons who judge of works of art simply and solely by the effect such works of art produce upon themselves, who, where they are stirred to pleasure, to reverence, or to laughter, are content to enjoy, to be reverent, or to laugh, without too close inquiry as to the means whereby their emotions are produced, with still less inquiry as to whether such means be legitimate or the reverse. I speak, therefore, not from the standpoint of the instructed critic, but from that of the public, more or less impressionable, more or less uneducated, upon whom the artist works; and it follows that when I speak of woman's inferiority to man in creative art I mean, not her inferiority in technique (whereon I am not competent to express opinion), but her incapacity to arouse in the ordinary human being such emotions of wonder, delight, and sorrow as men who have the requisite skill in creative art have power to arouse. I have thought it necessary to explain thus much lest my point of view be misunderstood, and I be credited with an attempt to usurp the functions of the trained critic.

Speaking, then, as one of the common herd — the public — I ask myself why it is that as a rule woman's art leaves me cold, woman's literature unconvinced, dissatisfied, and even irritated? And the only answer I can find is that they are artificial; that they are not a representation of life or beauty seen by a woman's eyes, but an attempt to render life or beauty as man desires that a woman should see and render it. The attempt is unconscious, no doubt; but it is there — thwarting, destroying, and annulling.

Perhaps it is necessary to be a woman oneself in order to understand how weak, false, and insincere is the customary feminine attempt at creative art. I do not think that a man can understand how bad most of our work in art and literature really is, for the simple reason that he cannot see the lie in it. He believes, for instance, that we are such creatures as we represent ourselves to be in most of the books we write; we only try to believe it. Wherein is all the difference between a blunder and a lie. We cannot even draw ourselves, our passions and emotions — because we are accustomed to look at ourselves, our passions and emotions, not with our own eyes, but through the spectacles with which he has provided us. When we come to portray our own hearts, it would seem that they are almost as much of a mystery to ourselves as they are to him; but then we are not striving to portray our own hearts, but to describe beings who shall be something like what we have been taught women ought to be, and to account for their actions by motives which we have been told ought to actuate them. Because we have been told that we are creatures existing only for love and maternity, we draw creatures existing only for love and maternity — and call them women. It is perfectly natural that men should draw such creatures; they could not very well draw anything else, for they see them like that. Their portraits are honest, if lop-sided; ours are lop-sided without being honest — the result of an attempt to see ourselves through another's eyes.

The point of view is everything. An artist is not to be blamed for his natural limitations, for his inability to see beyond his range of vision; but I am inclined to think that he ought to be execrated when he proceeds to stunt his powers by imposing unnatural limitations on himself. A man afflicted with a colour-blindness which leads him to turn out a portrait of me resplendent in beetroot hair and eyes of a vivid green cannot help himself. As he sees me, so he paints me; the effect may be curious but the thing itself is sincere. But that is no reason why artists endowed with normal vision should bind themselves down to slavish imitation of his peculiar colour-scheme. In the same way a person who is convinced that woman is a form of animated doll whereof the mechanism, when pressed on the right spot, squeaks out the two ejaculations of, 'I love you', and 'Oh, my dear baby', has a perfect right to describe her in those terms; but no woman has the right so to describe herself.

For countless generations the thoughts, the energies, and aspirations of woman have been concentrated upon love and maternity; yet how many are the works of art in which she has immortalised either passion which have endured because they were stamped with the impress of her own individuality and experience? For all that love is her whole existence, no woman has ever sung of love as man has sung of it, has painted it, has embodied it in drama. And of her attitude towards maternity what has she told us in her art? Practically nothing that is illuminating, that is not obvious, that has not been already said for her — usually much better than she herself can say it. As a matter of fact, her description of her emotions when she is in love or bears children is not, as a rule, a first-hand description; it is a more or less careful, more or less intelligent copy of the masculine conception of her emotions under those particular circumstances. Thus the business-like aspect of love in woman, the social or commercial necessity for sexual intercourse is usually ignored by an imitative feminine art — because it is lacking in man, and is, therefore, not really grasped by him. When he becomes aware of it he dislikes it — and draws a Becky Sharp (who has the secret sympathy of every woman not an heiress in her own right — if also the openly-expressed contempt).

Women who have treated of maternity in books or pictures have usually handled it in exactly the same spirit in which it is commonly handled by men — from what may be termed the conventional or Raphaelesque point of view. That is to say, they treat it from the superficial point of view of the outsider, the person who has no actual experience of the subject; yet even the most acid and confirmed of spinsters has an inside view of maternity unattainable by the most sympathetic and intuitive of men — since it has once been a possibility in her life. Yet from woman's art and woman's literature what does one learn of the essential difference between the masculine and feminine fashion of regarding that closest of all relations — the relation of mother and child?

I do not feel that I myself am qualified to define and describe that difference. It will have to be defined and described by a woman who has had experience of maternity; but at least I know that the difference exists. Men are capable of being both reverent and ribald on the subject of maternity; I have never met a woman who was either. (I have, of course, met one or two women who adopted the reverent pose; but in all such cases which have come within my experience it has been an undoubted pose, a more or less unconscious imitation of the reverent attitude in the men — usually husbands — with whom they came in contact.) For us the bearing of children is a matter far too serious to be treated with ribaldry; while as regards the lack of extreme reverence, it seems to me that it is impossible for any human being to revere — in the proper sense of the word — the performance by him or herself of a physical function. No doubt it will be objected that maternity has not only a physical aspect; to which I can only reply that it appears to be the purely physical aspect thereof which calls forth reverence and admiration in man. The typical duties of a mother to her children are often performed, as efficiently and as tenderly as any mother could perform them, by an aunt or a nurse; but they have never, when so performed, called forth the flood of idealism and admiration which has been lavished upon the purely physical relationship of mother and child as typified by a woman suckling her offspring. The sight of a mother so engaged has meant inspiration to a good many men; I may be wrong, but I do not imagine that it will ever mean real inspiration to any woman.

My own opinion — which I put forth in all diffidence, as one of the uninitiated — is, that while women, left to themselves, have considerably less reverence than men have for the physical aspect of maternity, they have a good deal more respect for its other aspects. Thus I have several times asked women whom I knew from the circumstances of their lives to have been exposed to temptation whether the thought that they might some day bear a child had not been a conscious, and not merely an instinctive, factor in their resistance to temptation and the restraint they had put upon their passions and emotions; and the reply has usually been in the affirmative. I do not know whether such a deliberate attitude towards the responsibilities of motherhood is general, but it seems to me essentially feminine, implying, as it does, the consciousness that it is not enough to bear a child, but that the child must be born of a clean body and come in contact with a clean mind — that the actual bringing of a new life into the world is only a small part of motherhood. It is the circumstances under which the child is born and the circumstances under which it is reared to which women attach infinitely more importance than men are apt to do; but, of course, where child-bearing is compulsory — and until very lately it has been practically compulsory upon all classes of wives — such an instinct does not get free play.

A good many times in my life I have heard the practice of passing the death sentence for the common crime of infanticide discussed by women, sometimes in an assemblage convened for the purpose, but more often where the subject has come up by chance. And I have always been struck by the attitude of the women who have discussed it — an attitude which, judged by the conventional or Raphaelesque standard, might be described as typically unfeminine and unmaternal — since their sympathies were invariably and unreservedly on the side of the erring mother, and I cannot remember having heard a single woman's voice raised in defence of the right to its life of the unwanted child. On the contrary, mothers of families, devoted to their own children and discharging their duties to them in a manner beyond reproach, have, in my hearing, not only pitied, but justified, the unfortunate creatures who, goaded by fear of shame and want of money, destroy the little life they themselves have given. That attitude seems to me to show that women recognise the comparative slightness of the mere physical tie, and that to them it is the other factors in the relationship of mother and child which really count — factors which have practically no chance of being brought into play in the case of the unwanted child.

It is eminently characteristic of the servile, and therefore imitative, quality of women's literature that the unwanted child — other than the illegitimate — has played practically no part in it. As long as child-bearing was an involuntary consequence of a compulsory trade — as, to a great extent, it still is — there must have been innumerable women who, year after year, bore children whom they did not desire to bear; who suffered the discomforts of pregnancy and the pangs of childbirth not that they might rejoice when a man was born into the world, but that a fresh and unwelcome burden might be added to their lives. And how unwelcome was that burden in many cases is proved by the voluntary and deliberate restriction of the modern family! Yet no woman, so far as I know, has ever taken up pen to write with truth and insight of this, the really tragic element in the life of countless wives — simply because man, not understanding, has never treated of it, because, in his ignorance, he has laid it down that woman finds instinctive and unending joy in the involuntary reproduction of her kind. One sees the advantage of such a comfortable belief to a husband disinclined to self-control.

Sixteen

If I have dwelt at some length upon woman's failure to achieve greatness in art and literature, it is because its art and literature reflect the inward life of a people, and the puny, trammelled and almost entirely imitative art of woman is a faithful reflection of the artificial habit and attitude of mind induced in her by the training for the married state, or its equivalent outside the law. As I have already said, the wonder is — when the tendency of that training is taken into account — not that she has done so little, but that she has done so much; for it must be borne in mind that as long as sexual love and maternity are in the slightest degree compulsory upon woman they can never prove to her the source of inspiration which they have so often proved to man. It is freedom and unfettered desire, not inevitable duty or the prospect of monetary gain, which awakens the creative instinct in humanity. The commercial element has always been incompatible with effective expression in art; no stockbroker, however exultant, has burst into lyric rhapsody over a rise in Home Rails, no grocer lifted up a psalm of praise because his till was full. It is because her love has always been her livelihood that woman has never been inspired by it as man has been inspired. And it is just because it is so business-like that her interest in love is often so keen. For instance, her customary appreciation of a book or a work of art dealing with love, and nothing but love, is the outcome of something more than sentiment and overpowering consciousness of sex. To her a woman in love is not only a woman swayed by emotion, but a human being engaged in carving for herself a career or securing for herself a means of livelihood. Her interest in a love story is, therefore, much more complex than a man's interest therein, and the appreciation which she brings to it is of a very different quality.

Love and maternity, then, have failed because of their compulsory character to inspire woman to artistic achievement; and from other sources of inspiration she has, as a rule, been debarred systematically. One hears, over and over again, of the artist who is inspired by the spirit of his time, who gives effective expression to the life and ideals of his time; and one remembers that man has always desired that woman should be debarred from contact with the life and spirit of the world in which she lived and moved and had her being, has always desired that she should drift and stagnate in a backwater of existence. The inspiration that springs from the sense of community, of fellowship, from enthusiasm for great interests shared with others was not to be for her; she was denied part or lot or interest in the making of contemporary history and to the passions enkindled by it she must be a stranger. Art has always responded to the uprush of a genuine popular enthusiasm, has embodied, shaped and moulded the ideas tossed about from mind to mind, and from man to man in a period of national effervescence and progress. The men who have left behind them an enduring name in the annals of art and literature were not unconscious of the life around them, were often enough caught up in the swirl of contemporary interests, and played an eager part in that making of contemporary history which we call politics. How many works of art do we not owe to the civic consciousness, to a man's pride in his own place, his desire to be worthy of it, his sense of comradeship and his glory in communal service? In every city worthy of the name, in every city that is anything more than an enlarged manufacturing slum, there stands, in brick or stone, some witness to the force and reality of the communal impulse in art. It was an impulse that seldom reached woman; who stood apart from the communal life, who knew not the service that brings with it sense of fellowship, who had not so much as a place to be proud of. Even today a woman takes her husband's nationality, and the place that was her own is hers no longer. She has drawn no inspiration from the thought that she is a citizen of no mean city.

We think of Milton as a poet; but to the men of his time he was something else. Twenty years of his life were given to politics and state-craft, and his verse is the product not only of his own genius, but of the national spirit of Puritanism — which was the desire to establish the kingdom of God upon earth. Dante, to us, is the man who ascended into heaven and descended into hell and wrote of what he saw; but it was not for these things, but for his partisanship of a losing cause, that he ate the bread of a stranger and found it salt. Few, if any, of the great ones of all time have stood apart in spirit from their own world with its hopes and its seething discontents; they spoke of it because they lived in it, loved it and wondered at it. It is significant that one of the few women whose written words have stood the test of centuries — St Teresa — was one whose aspirations were not narrowed to the duties of a husband's dwelling, who was passionately conscious of her part in the life of a great community, who made herself a power in the public life of the day — a woman capable of organisation and able to bend men and systems to an indomitable will.

My meaning, I hope, will not be misinterpreted or narrowed. I do not look upon the British House of Commons or the American House of Representatives, as at present instituted, as a likely forcing-ground for poets or composers; nor do I consider that no human being is qualified to produce a decent novel or paint a decent picture until his name is included in the electoral register. I have endeavoured to make it clear that it is not the letter of political life, but the spirit of a conscious communal life which kindles enthusiasm, arouses the desire of service and awakens art; that, as far as art is concerned, the important point is participation in ideas, not in elections. When women are informed that they cannot think publicly, or, as the cant phrase goes, think imperially, it should be borne in mind that public or imperial ideas have usually been labelled, 'For men only'.

There is, so far as I can see, no reason to suppose that the minds of women are naturally less accessible than the minds of men to the influence of what has been termed the crowd spirit. Such subordinate share as they have been permitted to take in the communal life of the various sects and churches they have availed themselves of to the full; at least they have understood the meaning of the term Communion of Saints. And the few women whose high birth has qualified them for the responsibilities of practical statesmanship, the guidance and governance of nations, have usually grasped their responsibilities with capability and understanding. Public spirit has been manifested in these exceptions to masculine rule as surely as it was manifested in the dreadful, hopeful crowd that once went marching to Versailles; and it has been written that if the men of the Paris Commune had espoused their cause with the desperate courage of the women, that cause had not been lost.

Seventeen

My object in writing so far has been to set forth the reasons for my belief that woman, as we know her to-day, is largely a manufactured product; that the particular qualities which are supposed to be inherent in her and characteristic of her sex are often enough nothing more than the characteristics of a repressed class and the entirely artificial result of her surroundings and training. I have tried to show that, given such surroundings and training, the ordinary or womanly woman was the kind of development to be expected; that even if it be the will of Providence that she should occupy the lower seat, man has actively assisted Providence by a resolute discouragement of her attempts to move out of it; and that it is impossible to say whether her typical virtues and her typical defects are inherent and inevitable, or induced and artificial, until she has been placed amidst other surroundings and subjected to the influence and test of a different system of education. Until such an experiment has been tried no really authoritative conclusion is possible; one can only make deductions and point to probabilities.

If, after four or five generations of freer choice and wider life, woman still persists in confining her steps to the narrow grooves where they have hitherto been compelled to walk; if she claims no life of her own, if she has no interests outside her home, if love, marriage and maternity is still her all in all; if she is still, in spite of equal education, of emulation and respect, the inferior of man in brain capacity and mental independence; if she still evinces a marked preference for disagreeable and monotonous forms of labour, for which she is paid at the lowest possible rate; if she still attaches higher value to the lifting of a top hat than to the liberty to direct her own life; if she is still untouched by public spirit, still unable to produce an art and a literature that is individual and sincere; if she is still servile, imitative, pliant — then, when those four or five generations have passed, the male half of humanity will have a perfect right to declare that woman is what he has always believed and desired her to be, that she is the chattel, the domestic animal, the matron or the mistress, that her subjection is a subjection enjoined by natural law, that her inferiority to himself is an ordained and inevitable inferiority. Then he will have that right, but not till then.

Some of us believe and hope with confidence that, given such wider life and freer choice, he would have to admit himself mistaken, would have to confess that the limitations once confining us were, for the most part, of his own invention. And we base that belief and very confident hope on the knowledge that there are in us, and in our sisters, many qualities which we are not supposed to possess and which once were unsuspected by ourselves; and on the certainty that the needs and circumstances of modern life are encouraging, whether or no we will it, the development of a side of our nature which we have heretofore been strictly forbidden to develop — the side that comes in contact with the world. Economic pressure and the law of self-preservation produced the 'womanly woman'; now, from the 'womanly woman' economic pressure and the law of self-preservation are producing a new type. It is no use for a bland and fatuous conservatism to repeat the parrot cry anent the sphere of woman being the home; we could not listen to its chirpings even if we would. For our stomachs are more insistent than any parrot cry, and they inform us that the sphere of woman, like the sphere of man, is the place where daily bread can be obtained.

There was a certain amount of truth in the formula once, in days when our social and industrial system was run on more primitive lines, when the factory was not, and the home was a place of trade and business as well as a place to live in. But the modern civilised home is, as a rule, and to all intents and purposes, only the shell of what it was before that revolution in industrial methods which began about the middle of the eighteenth century.

The alteration in the status and scope of the home is best

and most clearly typified by the divided life led by the modern trader, manufacturer or man of business; who, in the morning, arises, swallows his breakfast and goes forth to his shop, his factory or his office; and, his day's work done, returns to the suburban residence which it is the duty of his wife to look after, either personally or by superintendence of the labour of servants. His place of business and his place of rest and recreation are separate institutions, situated miles apart; the only connection between the two is the fact that he spends a certain portion of the day in each, and that one provides the money for the upkeep of the other. But his ancestor, if in the same line of business, had his place of money-making and his place of rest under the same roof, and both were comprehended in the meaning of the term 'home'. The primitive form of shop, though in gradual and inevitable process of extinction, is still plentiful enough in villages, in country towns and even in the by-streets of cities. It takes the shape of a ground-floor apartment in the proprietor's dwelling-house, provided with a counter upon which the customer raps, with a more or less patient persistence, with the object of arousing the attention of some member of the hitherto invisible household. Eventually, in response to the summons, a man, woman or child emerges from behind the curtained door which separates the family place of business from the family sitting-room, and proceeds to purvey the needful string, matches or newspapers. In such an establishment no outside labour is engaged, the business is carried on under the same roof as the home and forms an integral part of the duties of the home; it is a family affair giving a certain amount of employment to members of the family. And when, owing to the erection round the corner of a plate-glass-windowed establishment run on more business-like and attractive lines, it fails and has to put up its shutters, those members of the family who have been dependent on it for a livelihood will have to seek that livelihood elsewhere. The boy who has been accustomed to help his parents in looking after the shop, running errands and delivering orders, will have to turn to a trade, if he is to be sure of his bread; the girl who has been fulfilling duties of the same kind will have to enter domestic service, a factory or a shop in which she is a paid assistant. In other words, she, like her brother, will be driven out of the home because the home can no longer support her; and it can no longer support her because its scope has been narrowed. Formerly it had its bread-winning as well as its domestic side; now, as an inevitable consequence of the growth of collective industry, of specialisation and centralisation, the bread-winning or productive side has been absorbed, and nothing remains but the domestic or unproductive. And in the event of the failure of such a family business as I have described, the head of the household, however firmly convinced he might be that the true and only sphere of woman is the home, would probably do his level best to obtain for his daughter a situation and means of livelihood outside her proper sphere.

As an example of the tendency of the home to split up into departments I have instanced the familiar process of the disappearance of a small retail business, simply because it is familiar, and a case where we can see the tendency at work beneath our own eyes. But, as a matter of fact, the division of what was formerly the home into unproductive and productive departments, into domestic work and work outside the house, has been far less thorough and complete in the retail trade than in other spheres of labour. The factory, which has absorbed industry after industry formerly carried on in the house, is a comparatively modern institution; so is the bakehouse. Weaving and spinning were once domestic trades; so was brewing. Not so very long ago it was usual enough for the housewife, however well-to-do, to have all her washing done in her own home; not so very long ago she made her own pickles and her own jam. When the average household was largely self-supporting, producing food for its own consumption, and linen for its own wearing, it gave employment to many more persons than can be employed in it to-day. The women's industries of a former date have, for the most part, been swallowed by the factory. They were never industries at which she earned much money; so far as the members of a family were concerned they were rewarded with nothing more than the customary wage of subsistence; but — and this is the real point — they were industries at which woman not only earned her wage of subsistence, but indirectly a profit for her employer, the head of the household — the husband or father.

The displacement of labour which followed the adoption of

machinery in crafts and manufactures formerly carried on by hand affected the conditions of women's work just as it affected the work of men. Factories and workshops took the place of home industries; the small trader and the master-craftsman fell under the domination first of the big employer and later of the limited liability company. It was cheaper to produce goods in large quantities by the aid of machinery than in small quantities by hand; so the 'little man' who ran his own business with the aid of his own family, being without capital to expend on the purchase of machinery, was apt to find competition too much for him and descend to the position of a wage-earner. For woman the serious fact was that under the new system of collective industry and production on a large scale her particular sphere, the home, ceased to be self-supporting, since its products were under-sold by the products of the factory. Jam and pickles could be produced more cheaply in a factory furnished with vats than in a kitchen supplied with saucepans; it was more economical to buy bread than to bake it, because the most economical way of baking was to bake it in the mass. A man might esteem the accomplishment of pickle-making or linen-weaving as an excellent thing in woman; but unless expense was really no object he would not encourage his wife and daughters to excel in these particular arts, since it was cheaper to buy sheets and bottled onions round the corner than to purchase the raw material and set the female members of his family to work upon it. In the redistribution of labour which followed upon the new order of things man, not for the first time, had invaded the sacred sphere of woman and annexed a share thereof.

The natural and inevitable result of this new and improved state of things was that woman, deprived of the productive industries at which she had formerly earned her keep and something over for her employer, was no longer a source of monetary profit to that employer. On the contrary, so far as money went and so long as she remained in the home, she was often a distinct loss. Instead of baking bread for her husband or father, her husband or father had to expend his money on buying bread for her to eat; she no longer wove the material for other people's garments; on the contrary, the material for her own had to be obtained at the draper's. The position, for man, was a serious one;

for, be it remembered, he could not lower the wages of his domestic animal. These had always been fixed, whatever work she did, at the lowest possible rate — subsistence rate; so that even when her work ceased to be profitable her wages could not be made to go any lower — there was nowhere lower for them to go. One's daughter had to be fed, clothed and lodged even if the narrowed scope of the home provided her with no more lucrative employment than dusting china dogs on the mantelpiece.

Under these circumstances the daughters of a household found themselves, often enough, face to face with a divided duty: the duty of earning their keep, which would necessitate emergence from the home, and the duty of remaining inside the sacred sphere — and confining their energies to china dogs. Left to themselves the more energetic and ambitious would naturally adopt the first alternative, the more slothful and timid as naturally adopt the second; but they were not always left to themselves, nor were their own desires and predilections the sole factor in their respective decisions. The views of the head of the household, who now got little or no return for the outlay he incurred in supporting them, had also to be taken into consideration; and his views were usually influenced by the calls made upon his purse. Theoretically he might hold fast to the belief that woman's sphere was the home and nothing but the home. Actually he might object to the monetary outlay incurred if that belief was acted upon. The father of five strapping girls (all hungry several times a day), who might or might not succeed in inducing five desirable husbands to bear the expense of their support, would probably discover that, even if home was the sphere of woman, there were times when she was better out of it. It is a curious fact that when women are blamed for intruding into departments of the labour market hitherto reserved for men, the abuse which is freely showered upon the intruders is in no wise poured forth upon the male persons appertaining to the said intruders — who have presumably neglected to provide the funds necessary to enable their female relations to pass a blameless, if unremunerative, existence making cakes for home consumption or producing masterpieces in Berlin wool-work. The different treatment meted out to the guilty parties in this respect seems to be another example of the practice of apportioning blame only to the person least able to resent it. It is quite natural that man should refuse to support healthy and able-bodied females; but he must not turn round and be nasty when, as a direct consequence of his refusal, the healthy and able-bodied females endeavour to support themselves.

For good or for evil a good many millions of us have been forced out of the environment which we once believed to be proper to our sex; and to our new environment we have to adapt ourselves — if we are to survive. Work in the factory or in the office, work which brings us into contact with the outside world, calls for the exercise of qualities and attainments which we had no need of before, for the abandonment of habits and ideas which can only hamper our progress in our changed surroundings. Our forefathers — those, at any rate, of the upper and middle class — admired fragility of health in woman; and, in order to please them, our foremothers fell in with the idea and appealed to the masculine sense of chivalry by habitual indulgence in complaints known as swoons and vapours. Persons subject to these tiresome and inconvenient diseases would stand a very poor chance of regular and well-paid employment as teachers, sanitary inspectors, journalists and typists; so teachers, sanitary inspectors, journalists and typists have repressed the tendency to swoons and vapours. In these classes an actual uncertainty prevails as to the nature of vapours, and swooning is practically a lost art. Instead of applying their energies to the cultivation of these attractive complaints, working and professional women are inclined to encourage a condition of rude bodily health which stands them in good stead in their work, and is, therefore, a valuable commercial asset.

Just as we have been forced by contact with the outside world to cultivate not weakness but health, so by the same contact we have been forced to cultivate not folly but intelligence. The silly angel may be a success in the home; she is not a success in trade or business. Man may desire to clasp her and kiss her and call her his own; but there are moments when he tires of seeing her make hay of his accounts and correspondence. His natural predilection for her type may, and often does, induce him to give her the preference over her fellows in business matters; but he usually ends by admitting that, for certain purposes at least, the human being with brains is preferable to the seraph without them. It has been borne in upon the modern woman that it pays her to have brains — even although they must be handled very cautiously for fear of wounding the susceptibilities of her master. She learned that lesson not in her own sphere, but in the world outside it; and it is a lesson that has already had far-reaching consequences. Having, in the first instance, acquired a modicum of intelligence because she had to, she is now acquiring it in larger quantities because she likes it. The trades which do not require the qualification of stupidity are counteracting the effect upon her of the trade which did — the compulsory trade of marriage.

Eighteen

If the division of the home, and the inevitable consequences that followed on that division, had done nothing more than teach some of us to value our health and respect our brains we should have very good cause to bless the break-up of that overestimated institution. But, as a matter of fact, our contact with the wider world is doing a great deal more for us than that. It is testing our powers in new directions; it is bringing new interests into our lives; it is teaching us how very like we are unto our brothers — given similar environment; and, most important of all, it is sweeping away with a steady hand that distrust and ignorance of each other which was alike the curse and the natural result of age-long isolation in the home and immemorial training in the service, not of each other, but only of our masters.

It may be true that women in general once disliked and meanly despised each other. At any rate, man has always desired that it should be true; so, the aim and object of woman's life being the gratification of his desires, such mutual dislike and contempt was no doubt cultivated and affected by her. But if it was true once, it is not true now; except, maybe, amongst the silly angel class — a class already growing rarer, and soon, one hopes, to be well on the way to extinction. The working-woman, the woman with wider interests than her mother's, in learning to respect herself is learning to respect her counterpart — the human being, like unto herself, who, under the same disadvantages fights the same battle as her own. And recognising the heaviness, the unfairness of those disadvantages, she recognises the bond of common interest that unites her to her sister. In short, for the first time in her history she is becoming actively class-conscious.

We speak best of that which we have seen with our own eyes

and heard with our own ears; therefore I make no excuse for obtruding my personal experiences in this connection. For many years the women who came into my life intimately and closely were, with few exceptions, women who had to work — journalists, artists, typists, dressmakers, clerks; practically all of them dependent on their own work and practically all of them poor — some bitterly poor. And that class, because I know it so well, I have learned to respect. It is a class which has few pleasures in life, because it has so little money to spend on them; which, as a rule, works harder than a man would work in the same position, because its pay is less; which is not unexposed to temptation, but holds temptation as a thing to be resisted; yet which is tolerant to those who fail under it, knowing the excuse to be made for them. The woman belonging to that class does not turn away from the sinner who walks the street with a painted face; likely enough she remembers that she, too, was brought up to believe that the awakening of sexual desire must be her means of livelihood, and she knows that, if she had not cast that belief behind her, she, too, when need pressed upon her, might have walked the streets for hire. Wherefore she is more inclined to say to herself, 'But for the grace of God, there go I'. She has learned to know men as the sheltered woman seldom knows them; to know more of the good in them, more of the ill; she has met and talked with them without compliment and without ceremony; has taken orders from and been rebuked by them; has been to them fellow-worker and sometimes friend; has sometimes met and fought the brute in them. In the same way she has worked with women and learned to know them; and the result of her experience is, that she has lost any natural distrust of her own sex which she may once have possessed; has come to rely upon her own sex for the help which she herself is willing enough to render. The sense of a common interest, the realisation of common disabilities, have forced her into class-consciousness and partisanship of her class. I know many women of the type I have described — women who have gone through the mill, some married, some unmarried. And of them all I know hardly one whose life is not affected, to an appreciable extent, by the sense of fellowship with her sisters.

The average man, it seems to me, fails utterly to realise how strong this sense of fellowship, of trade unionism, can be in us; he has (as I have already pointed out) explained away its manifestations in the match-making industry by accounting for them on other grounds. He has forgotten that it was a woman who, for the sake, not of a man, but of another woman, went out into a strange land, saying, 'Whither thou goest I will go; thy people shall be my people and thy God my God'. To him, one imagines, that saying must always have been a dark one; to us there seems nothing strange in it.

A friend of my own (who will forgive me for repeating her confidence) told me the other day of a happening in her life that, to my mind, exactly illustrates the awakening of class-consciousness amongst women. It was the careless speech of a man, addressed to her while she was still a very young girl, to the effect that all women over fifty should be shot. The words were lightly spoken, of course, and were probably intended half as a compliment to her manifest youth; certainly they were not intended as an insult. But their effect was to rouse in her a sense of insult and something akin to a passion of resentment that she and her like should only be supposed to exist so long as they were pleasing, only so long as they possessed the power of awakening sexual desire. She took them as an insult to herself because they were an insult to women in general; and, lightly spoken as they were, they made upon her an impression which helped to mould her life.

I give my friend's experience because it seems to me to be typical; because amongst women of my own class I know others who have felt the same rush of anger at the revelation of a similar attitude towards the sex they belong to; who have raged inwardly as they recognised that character, worth, intellect were held valueless in woman, that nothing counted in her but the one capacity — the power of awaking desire. That is an attitude which we who have become conscious of our class resent with all our souls; since we realise that to that attitude on the part of man, to compliance with it on the part of woman, we owe the degradation of our class.

Most important of all, the knowledge of each other and the custom and necessity of working side by side in numbers is bringing with it the consciousness of a new power — the power of organisation. It is a power that we have hitherto lacked, not because we were born without the seed of it in our souls, but because our fenced-in, isolated lives have given small opportunity for its growth and development. And it is a power which we are now acquiring because we have been forced to recognise the need of it, because we can no longer do without it. It is being borne in on us that if we are to have fair play, if our wages are to rise above subsistence point, if we are to be anything more than hewers of wood, drawers of water, and unthinking reproducers of our kind, we have to stand together; that if we are to have any share of our own in the world into which we were born, if our part in it is to be anything more than that of the beggar with outstretched hand awaiting the crumbs that fall from another's table, we have to work together. And it is work in the mill, the factory, the office that is teaching us the lesson of public spirit, of combination for a common purpose — a lesson that was never taught us in the home where we once lived narrowly apart.

Nineteen

If what I have written has any truth in it, I have shown that we have good grounds for believing that the degradation of woman's position and the inferiority of woman's capacities are chiefly due to the compulsory restriction of her energies and ambitions to the uncertain livelihood and ill-paid trade of marriage. I have shown that the trade is ill paid simply because it is largely compulsory; that, in accordance with economic law, the wife and mother will be held cheap for just so long as she is a drug in the market. I have shown how the unsatisfactory position of the wife and mother, the unsatisfactory training to which she has been subjected from her childhood up, affects the earning and productive powers of woman in those other occupations which the change in social and industrial conditions has forced her to adopt; and I have shown how the new influences engendered by her new surroundings are gradually and inevitably counteracting the peculiar habit of mind acquired in the narrow precincts of the home. It remains to be considered how far these influences are reaching and affecting the life of the home itself — how far they are likely to improve the position not only of the woman who earns her own wage and directs her own life, but of the woman who has no means of augmenting the low remuneration which is at present considered sufficient for the duties of a wife and mother.

I suppose that in the recent history of woman nothing is more striking than the enormous improvement that has taken place in the social position of the spinster. In many ranks of life the lack of a husband is no longer a reproach; and some of us are even proud of the fact that we have fought our way in the world without aid from any man's arm. At any rate, we no longer feel it necessary to apologise for our existence; and when we are assured that we have lost the best that life has to offer us, we are not unduly cast down. (I am speaking, of course, of the independent woman with an interest in life and in herself; not of the poor, mateless product of the tradition that we exist only to awaken desire in man. There are still many such, no doubt — the victims of a servile training. On whom may God have mercy — man having no use for them and they none for themselves!) By sheer force of self-assertion we have lifted ourselves from the dust where we once crawled as worms and no women; we no longer wither on the virgin thorn — we flourish on it; and, ungarnished though we be with olive-boughs, we are not ashamed when we meet with our enemies in the gate.

So far as I can see, nothing like the same improvement has taken place in recent years in the position of the average married woman. So far as I can see, the average husband, actual or to be, still entertains the conviction that the word helpmeet, being interpreted, means second fiddle; and acts in accordance with that honest conviction. He still feels that it is the duty of his wife to respect him on the ground that he did not happen to be born a woman; he still considers it desirable that the mother of his children should not be over wise. He still clings to the idea that a wife is a creature to be patronised; with kindness, of course — patted on the head, not thumped — but still patronised. While he is yet unmated his dream of the coming affinity still takes the shape of some one smaller than himself who asks him questions while he strokes her hair. On the whole, therefore, he tends to avoid marriage with those women who are not fit subjects for patronage — who, be it noted, also tend to avoid marriage with him; and thus, in the natural order of things, the average wife is the person who is willing to submit to be patronised. I do not mean that there are not many exceptions to this rule; but they are exceptions. And it is obvious that human beings, men or women, who consider themselves fit subjects for patronage are not those who make for progress or possess any very great power of improving their own status.

Myself I have not the least doubt that such improvement as has already been effected in the status of the wife and mother has originated outside herself, and is, to a great extent, the work of the formerly condemned spinster. I do not mean that the spinster has always laboured to that end intentionally; I mean, rather, that as she improves her own position, as she takes advantage of its greater freedom, its less restricted opportunities, its possibilities of pleasing herself and directing her own life, she inevitably, by awaking her envy, drags after her the married woman who once despised her and whose eyes she has opened to the disadvantages of her own dependent situation. It is the independent woman with an income, earned or unearned, at her own disposal, with the right to turn her energies into whatever channel may seem good to her, who is steadily destroying the prestige of marriage; and the prestige of marriage has hitherto been an important factor in the eagerness of women for matrimony. Once it has gone, once it makes absolutely no difference to the esteem in which a woman is held, whether she is called Mrs or whether she is called Miss, a new inducement will have to be found, at any rate for the woman who is not obliged to look upon marriage as a means of providing her with bread and butter. Such women will require some additional advantage to replace the social prestige to which they no longer attach any value — that is to say, as a condition of becoming wives and mothers, they will require their status to be raised; and their action in raising their own status will tend to raise the status of married women in general.

Not very long ago, in one of the columns which a daily paper was devoting to animated correspondence dealing with the rights and wrongs of an agitation carried on by women, I came across a brief contribution to the discussion which furnished me with considerable food for thought. It was a letter written by a palpably infuriated gentleman, who denounced the agitation in question as the outcome of the unmarried woman's jealousy of the privileges of her married sister. This very masculine view of the controversy had never struck me before; and, being a new idea to me, I sat down to consider whether it was in any way justified by facts.

The first step, naturally, was to ascertain what were the special privileges which were supposed to arouse in those deprived of them a sense of maddened envy. On this point I did not rely solely on my own conclusions; I consulted, at various times, interested friends, married and unmarried; with the result that I have ascertained the privileges of the married woman to be, at the outside, three in number. (About two of them there is no doubt; the third is already being invaded, and can no longer be esteemed the exclusive property of the matron.) They are as follows:

1. The right to wear on the third finger of the left hand a gold ring of approved but somewhat monotonous pattern.
2. The right to walk in to dinner in advance of women unfurnished with a gold ring of the approved, monotonous pattern.
3. The right of the wife and mother to peruse openly and in the drawing-room certain forms of literature — such as French novels of an erotic type — which the ordinary unmarried woman is supposed to read only in the seclusion of her bedroom.

I cannot honestly say that any one of these blessings arouses in me a spasm of uncontrollable envy, a mad desire to share in it at any cost. As a matter of fact, I have — like many of my unmarried friends — annexed one of the above matrimonial privileges, if not in deed, at any rate potentially and in thought. I have never yet felt the desire to study French novels of an erotic type; but if I ever do feel it, I shall have no hesitation in perusing them in public — even on the top of a bus.

One does not imagine that the mere wearing of a plain gold ring would in itself awaken perfervid enthusiasm in any woman of ordinary intelligence; nor does one imagine that any woman of ordinary intelligence would be greatly elated or abashed by entering a dining-room first or seventh — provided, of course, that the table was furnished with enough food to go round. One feels that these temptations are hardly glittering enough to entice reluctant woman into marriage. That there has been a social pressure which has impelled her into it I have not denied; on the contrary, I have affirmed it. But that social pressure has not taken the form of a passionate desire for one or two small and formal distinctions, but of a fear of spinsterhood with its accompaniments, scorn and confession of failure in your trade. And as spinsterhood grows more enviable, so does the fear of it grow less.

It may be objected that in my brief list of the matron's privileges I have omitted the most important of them all — motherhood.

I have done so deliberately and for two reasons — because under any system of more or less compulsory marriage there must always be an appreciable number of wives who look upon motherhood rather as a burden than as a privilege; and because motherhood does not appertain exclusively to the married state. There is such a thing as an illegitimate birth-rate.

I myself am far from desiring that the wife and mother should not possess privileges; it seems to me that the work of a woman who brings up children decently, creditably, and honourably is of such immense importance that it ought to be suitably rewarded. (That, of course, is a very different thing from admitting that a person who has gone through a ceremony which entitles her to hold sexual intercourse with another person is thereby entitled to consider herself my superior.) But I am very certain that it never will be suitably rewarded until it is undertaken freely and without pressure, and until the wife and mother herself summons up courage to insist on adequate payment for her services. It may not be necessary that that payment should be made in actual money; but, in whatever form it is made, it must be of a more satisfactory and substantial nature than the present so-called privileges of the married woman, involving an all-round improvement in her status. And that all-round improvement she will demand — and get — only when it is borne in upon her that her unmarried sisters have placed themselves in a position to get out of life a great deal more than she is permitted to get out of it. When she realises that fact to the full she will go on strike — and good luck to her!

Meanwhile, it seems to me that there is something more than a little pathetic in the small airs of superiority which are still affected by the average unintelligent matron towards her husbandless sister. Personally I always feel tender towards these little manifestations of the right to look down on the 'incomplete', the unconsciously servile imitation of the masculine attitude in this respect. You watch the dull lives that so many of these married women lead, you realise the artificial limitations placed upon their powers, you pity them for the sapping of individuality which is the inevitable result of repression of their own and unquestioning acceptance of other people's opinions, for the cramping of their interests, perhaps for the necessity of cultivating the animal side of their natures — and you do not grudge them such small compensations as come their way. It will be better for them and for their children when they realise in what this fancied superiority of the married woman consists; but meanwhile let them enjoy it.

Only a little while past I met a perfect example of this tendency on the part of a married woman to plume herself on marriage as a virtue — or rather, I met her again. She had been my friend once — several years ago — and I had liked her for her intelligence, her humour, her individual outlook on life. We knew each other well for some months, then we were separated, and she wrote to me that she was getting married; and with her marriage she gave up professional work and passed out of my life. I heard little and saw nothing of her for years, until she wrote that she was staying near me and would like us to meet again. I went, and she told me what her life had been since she married. It was a story that I can only call foul — of insult, brutality, and degradation. What sickened me about it was the part that remained unspoken — the thought that the woman I once knew, clean, high-minded, and self-respecting, should have consented to stand for so long in the relation of wife to such a man as she described. One could see what contact with him had done for her; it had dragged her down morally and spiritually; the pitch had defiled her. She had, I knew, a small income of her own — sufficient to live upon without having recourse to her husband — so I urged her bluntly to leave him. She refused, crying feebly; made the usual rejoinder of weak-minded married women run into a corner — that I was not married myself and could not understand; and spent another hour bewailing her lot with tears. I saw that her courage and character had been sapped out of her, that it was no use appealing to what she no longer possessed, and that all she asked was sympathy of the type that listens with an occasional pat on the shoulder or soothing stroke on the arm; so I gave of it, in silence, as well as I could. At the end of a good hour she dried her tears, and declared that she was selfish to talk about nothing but herself, that she must hear my news and what I had been doing. I did not like to refuse, for I thought it better to turn her thoughts away from her troubles, if only for a little; besides, she had liked me genuinely once, and

I think her interest in me was still genuine. But as I complied and talked to her about myself, I felt miserably ashamed. For, as it happened, I was very happy then — happier, in some ways, than I had ever been in my life, since, almost for the first time in my life, I had learned the meaning of good luck. I thought of all the kindness, the friendliness, the consideration that was being shown to me — I thought of my work and my pleasure in it — of my interest in work done with others and the sense of comradeship it brings. And I thought how the poor soul who had wept her handkerchief into a rag must realise the contrast of our two lives, must feel how unjust it was that one woman should have so little and another have so much. So, as I say, I felt ashamed, and talked on, conscious of mental discomfort, until I saw her looking at me thoughtfully, as if she were about to speak. I stopped to hear what she had to say; and it was this:

'I suppose you will never marry now?'

For a moment I did not see the real purport of the question, and I dare say I looked astonished as I answered that it was most unlikely, and I had no thought of it. She surveyed me steadily, to make sure that I was speaking the truth; then, having apparently convinced herself that I was, she sighed.

'It is a pity. Every woman ought to get married. Your life isn't complete without it. It is an experience . . . .'

Those, as far as I remember, were the exact words she used. (There is no danger that she will ever read them.) They left me dumb; their unconscious irony was so pathetic and so dreadful. Marriage an experience — it had been one for her! And 'your life isn't complete without it.' This from a woman whose husband had threatened to knock pieces out of her with a poker! The situation seemed to me beyond tears and beyond laughter — the poor, insulted, bullied thing, finding her one source of pride in the fact that she had experienced sexual intercourse. If there had been a child I could have understood; but there had, I think, never been a child — at any rate, there was not one living. If there had been, I believe I should have said to her what was in my mind — for the child's sake; I should have hated to think of it growing up in that atmosphere, in its mother's squalid faith in the essential glory of animalism. But as there was no child, and as she was so dulled, so broken, I said nothing. It was all she had

139

— the consciousness that she, from her vantage-ground of completeness and experience, had the right to look down on me — on one of the unmarried, a woman who 'could not understand'. It was her one ewe-lamb of petty consolation; and I had not the heart to try and take it from her.

Twenty

My intention in writing this book has not been to inveigh against the institution of marriage, the life companionship of man and woman; all that I have inveighed against has been the largely compulsory character of that institution — as far as one-half of humanity is concerned — the sweated trade element in it, and the glorification of certain qualities and certain episodes and experiences of life at the expense of all the others. I believe — because I have seen it in the working — that the companionship in marriage of self-respecting man and self-respecting woman is a very perfect thing; but I also believe that, under present conditions, it is not easy for self-respecting woman to find a mate with whom she can live on the terms demanded by her self-respect. Hence a distinct tendency on her part to avoid marriage. Those women who look at the matter in this light are those who, while not denying that matrimony may be an excellent thing in itself, realise that there are some excellent things which may be bought too dear. That is the position of a good many of us in these latter days. If we are more or less politely incredulous when we are informed that we are leading an unnatural existence, it is not because we have no passions, but because life to us means a great deal more than one of its possible episodes. If we decline to listen with becoming reverence to disquisitions on the broadening effect of motherhood upon our lives, the deep and miraculous understanding that it brings into our hearts, it is not because we are contemptuous of maternity, but because we have met so many silly persons who brought babies into the world and remained just as silly as they were before. We are quite aware, too, that it is, for the most part, women of our own unmated class, and, likely enough, of our own way of thinking, who spend their days in teaching bungling mothers how to rear the children who would otherwise only come into the world in order to afford employment to the undertaker by going out of it. (A considerable proportion of the infant population of this country would be in a parlous state if the 'superfluous women' thereof were suddenly caught up into the air and dumped *en bloc* in the Sahara.)

And in this connection I feel it necessary to state that I have hitherto sought in vain in real life for that familiar figure in fiction — the unmarried woman whose withered existence is passed in ceaseless and embittered craving for the possession of a child of her own. The sufferings of this unfortunate creature, as depicted by masculine writers, have several times brought me to the verge of tears; it is difficult to believe that they are entirely the result of a vivid masculine imagination; but honesty compels me to admit that I have never discovered their counterpart in life, in spite of the fact that my way has led me amongst spinsters of all ages. Young unmarried women have told me frankly that they would like to bear a child; a very few elderly unmarried women have told me that they would have preferred to marry; and quite a number of married women have told me that they should have done better for themselves by remaining single. I have known wives who desired maternity as anxiously as others desired to avoid it; but the spinster whose days are passed in gloomy contemplation of her lack of olive-branches I have not yet met. I started by believing in her, just as I started by believing that the world held nothing for me but marriage and reproduction of my kind. Later on I discovered that there were more things in heaven and earth than marriage and reproduction of my kind, and I have no reason to suppose that I am the only woman who has made that discovery.

The women I have known who lamented their single state as a real evil have been actuated in their dislike of it by mixed motives. A desire to bear children has, perhaps, been one; but it has always been interwoven with the desire to improve their position socially or commercially, and the corresponding fear of failure or poverty implied by spinsterhood. So far as my experience goes, the only women who fret passionately at the lack of children of their own are married women whose husbands are desirous of children.

I should be the last to deny that many unmarried women have the sense of maternity strongly developed; but the sense of maternity, as I see it, is not completely dependent on the accidents of marriage and childbirth. As I have already said, I believe it is not the physical side of maternity — the side which appeals so strongly to men — which appeals most strongly to women; and from the other, and, to me, infinitely more beautiful side, no unmarried woman is necessarily debarred. The spinster who devotes herself to permanent lamentation over her lack of descendants must (if she exists) be a person who has never risen above the male conception of motherhood as a physical and instinctive process. Some of the best mothers I have met have never borne a child; but one does not imagine that it will be counted to them for unrighteousness that the children who rise up and call them blessed are not their own. Nor is it childhood alone which enkindles the sense of maternity in women; the truest mother I know is one who enwraps with her love a 'child' who came into the world before she was thought of.

After all, there is a kinship that is not that of the flesh, and some of us are very little the children of our parents. The people who have framed and influenced the conditions under which we live, whose thoughts have moulded our lives, have also had a share in our making. It is possible that descendants of Homer walk the earth to-day — very worthy persons whose existence is of no particular moment to any but themselves. Shakespeare was married I know, and I believe he was the father of a family; but of how many that family consisted, what were their names and what became of them all, I have never even troubled to inquire. Did Goethe leave descendants, or did he not? I frankly confess that I don't know, simply because I have never had the slightest curiosity on the subject. But Faust has been part of my life. It matters very little to the world at large what became of the children whom Jean Jacques Rousseau handed over to the tender mercies of a foundling hospital; but there are very few people alive to-day to whom it does not matter that the current of the world's striving was turned into a new channel by the spiritual sons of Rousseau — the men who made the French Revolution. Reproduction is not everything; the men and women who have striven to shorten the hours of child-labour have often been possessed of a keener sense of responsibility and tenderness, a keener sense of fatherhood and motherhood, than the parents whose children they sought to protect. If I were one of those who have so striven, I should consider that the help I had given to the world was no less worthy of honour and commendation than that of the paterfamilias who marches a family of fourteen to church on Sundays. If humanity had only been created in order to reproduce its kind, we might still be dodging cave-bears in the intervals of grubbing up roots with our nails. It is not only the children who matter: there is the world into which they are born. Every human being who influences for the better, however slightly, the conditions under which he lives is doing something for those who come after; and thus, it seems to me, that those women who are proving by their lives that marriage is not a necessity for them, that maternity is not a necessity for them, are preparing a heritage of fuller humanity for the daughters of others — who will be daughters of their own in the spirit, if not in the flesh. The home of the future will be more of an abiding-place and less of a prison because they have made it obvious that, so far as many women are concerned, the home can be done without; and if the marriage of the future is what it ought to be — a voluntary contract on both sides — it will be because they have proved the right of every woman to refuse it if she will, by demonstrating that there are other means of earning a livelihood than bearing children and keeping house. It is the woman without a husband to support her, the woman who has no home but such as she makes for herself by her own efforts, who is forcing a reluctant masculine generation to realise that she is something more than the breeding factor of the race. By her very existence she is altering the male conception of her sex.

According to latter-day notions, to speak in praise of celibacy in man or in woman is tantamount to committing the crime of high treason against the race. Other centuries — some of them with social systems quite as scientific as our own — have not been of that way of thinking; and one is half inclined to suspect that the modern dislike of the celibate has its root in the natural annoyance of an over-sexed and mentally lax generation at receiving ocular demonstration of the fact that the animal passions can be kept under control. It saves such a lot of trouble to assume at once that they cannot be kept under control; so, in place of the priest, we have the medicine man, whose business it is to make pathological excuses for original sin. Myself I have a good deal of respect for the celibate; not because he has no children, but because he is capable of self-control — which is a thing respectable in itself.

At the same time, I do not advocate celibacy except for persons whom it suits; but I do not see why persons whom it does suit should be ashamed of acknowledging the fact. I am inclined to think that they are more numerous than is commonly supposed, and I will admit frankly that I am exceedingly glad that it seems, in these latter days, to suit so many women. I am glad, not because the single life appears to me essentially better than the married, but because I believe that the conditions of marriage, as they affect women, can only be improved by the women who do without marriage — and do without it gladly. Other generations have realised that particular duties could best be performed by persons without engrossing domestic interests; and I believe that the wives and mothers of this generation require the aid of women unhampered by such interests — women who will eventually raise the value of the wife and mother in the eyes of the husband and father by making it clear to him that she did not enter the married state solely because there was nothing else for her to do, and that his child was not born simply because its mother had no other way of earning a living. There are women married every day, there are children born every day, for no better reasons than these.

Twenty-one

And the husband and father? What does he stand to gain or lose by that gradual readjustment of the conditions inside the home which must inevitably follow on the improvement of woman's position outside the home, the recognition of her right to an alternative career and the consequent discovery that she can be put to other uses than sexual attraction and maternity? How will he be affected by the fact that marriage has become a voluntary trade?

So far as one can see, he stands to lose something of his comfortable pride in his sex, his aristocratic pleasure in the accident of his birth, his aristocratic consciousness that deference is due to him merely because he was born in the masculine purple. The woman who has established her claim to humanity will no longer submit herself to the law of imposed stupidity; so the belief in her inherent idiocy will have to go, along with the belief in his own inherent wisdom. No longer will he take his daily enjoyment in despising the wife of his bosom — because nature has decreed that she shall be the wife of his bosom and not the wife of some one else's. There will be a readjustment of the wage-scale, too — a readjustment of the conditions of labour. With better conditions available outside the home, the wife and mother — no longer under the impression that it is a sin to think and a shame to be single — will decline to work inside the home for a wage that can go no lower, will decline to take all the dirty, monotonous and unpleasant work merely because her husband prefers to get out of it. She will agree that it is quite natural that he should dislike such dirty, monotonous or unpleasant toil; but she will point out to him that it is also quite natural that she should dislike it. And one imagines that they will come to a compromise. So far, under a non-compulsory marriage system, he would stand to lose; but, on the other hand, he would stand to gain — greatly.

He could be reasonably sure that his wife married him because she wanted to marry him, not because no other trade was open to her, not because she was afraid of being jeered and sneered at as an old maid. That in itself would be an advantage substantial enough to outweigh some loss of sex dignity. For it would be only his sense of sex dignity that would be impaired; his sense of personal dignity would be enhanced by the knowledge that he was a matter not of necessity but of choice. His wife's attitude towards him would be a good deal less complimentary to his class, but a good deal more complimentary to himself. The attitude of the girl who would 'marry any one to get out of this' is by no means complimentary to her future husband.

The fact that, under a voluntary system of marriage, he would have to pay, either in money or some equivalent of money, for work which he now gets done for nothing — and despises accordingly — would also bring with it a compensatory advantage. Woman's work in the home is often enough inefficient simply because it is sweated; there is a point at which cheap labour tends to become inefficient, and therefore the reverse of cheap; and that point appears to have been reached in a good many existing homes.

There is, it seems to me, another respect in which man, as well as woman, would eventually be the gainer by the recognition of woman's right to humanity on her own account. The custom of regarding one half of the race as sent into the world to excite desire in the other half does not appear to be of real advantage to either moiety, in that it has produced the over-sexed man and the over-sexed woman, the attitude of mind which sneers at self-control. Such an attitude the establishment of marriage for woman upon a purely voluntary basis ought to go far to correct; since it is hardly conceivable that women, who have other careers open to them and by whom ignorance is no longer esteemed as a merit, will consent to run quite unnecessary risks from which their unmarried sisters are exempt. When the intending wife and mother no longer considers it her duty to be innocent and complacent, the intending husband and father will learn, from sheer necessity, to see more virtue in self-restraint. With results beneficial to the race — and incidentally to himself. Humanity would seem to have paid rather a heavy price for that feminine habit of turning a blind eye to evil which it dignifies by the name of innocence.

I have sufficient faith in my brethren to be in no wise alarmed by dismal prophecies of their rapid moral deterioration when our helplessness and general silliness no longer make a pathetic appeal to their sense of pity and authority. No doubt the consciousness of superiority is favourable to the cultivation of certain virtues — the virtues of the patron; just as the consciousness of inferiority is favourable to the cultivation of certain other virtues — the virtues of the patronised. But I will not do my brother the injustice of believing that the virtues of the patron are the only ones he possesses; on the contrary, I have found him to be possessed of many others, have seen him just to an equal, courteous and considerate to those whom he had no reason to pity or despise. When the ordinary man and the ordinary wife no longer stand towards each other in the attitude of patron and patronised the virtues of both will need overhauling — that is all.

Nor does one see how the advancement of marriage to the position of a voluntary trade can work for anything but good upon the children born of marriage. Motherhood can be sacred only when it is voluntary, when the child is desired by a woman who feels herself fit to bear and to rear it; the child who is born because of his mother's inability to earn her bread by any trade but marriage, because of his mother's fear of the social disgrace of spinsterhood, has no real place in the world. He comes into it simply because the woman who gives him life was less capable or less courageous than her sisters; and it is not for such reasons that a man should be born.

And I fail to see that a future generation will be in any way injured because the mothers of that generation are no longer required to please their husbands by stunting and narrowing such brains as they were born with, because ignorance and silliness are no longer considered essential qualifications for the duties of wifehood and motherhood. The recognition of woman's complete humanity, apart from husband or lover, must mean inevitably the recognition of her right to develop every side of that humanity, the mental and moral, as well as the physical and sexual; and inevitably and insensibly the old aristocratic masculine cruelty which, because she was an inferior, imposed stupidity upon her and made lack of intelligence a preliminary condition of motherhood, will become a thing of the past. Nor will a man be less fitted to fight the battle of life with honour and advantage to himself, because he was not born the son of a fool.

The male half of creation is still apt to talk (if not quite so confidently as of yore) as if the instinct and desire for maternity were the one overpowering factor in our lives. It may be so as regards the majority of us, though the shrinkage of the birth-rate in so far as it is attributable to women would seem to point the other way; but, as I have shown, it is impossible to be certain on the point until other instincts and desires have been given fair play. Under a voluntary system of marriage they would be given fair play; in a world where a woman might make what she would of her own life, might interest herself in what seemed good to her, she would hardly bear a child unless she desired to bear it. That is to say, she would bear a child not just because it was the right thing for her to do — since there would be a great many other right things for her to do — but because the maternal instinct was so strong in her that it overpowered other interests, desires or ambitions, because she felt in her the longing to give birth to a son of whom she had need. And such a son would come into a world where his place was made ready for him; being welcome, and a hundred times welcome, because he was loved before he was conceived.

Nor does one imagine that such a son, when he grew of an age to understand, would think the less of his mother because he knew that he was no accident in her life, but a choice; because he learned that his birth was something more than a necessary and inevitable incident in her compulsory trade. One does not imagine that he would reverence her the less because he saw in her not only the breeding factor in the family, but a being in all respects as human as himself, who had suffered for him and suffered of her own free will; nor that he would be less grateful to her because she, having the unquestioned right to hold life from him, had chosen instead to give it.

ELIZABETH ROBINS
The Convert
Introduced by Jane Marcus

If you have enjoyed reading *Marriage as a Trade* we can also recommend *The Convert*, a novel written by Elizabeth Robins, a contemporary of Cicely Hamilton.

The Convert is a most readable novel in the Edwardian style: long, detailed, lots of plot, character development and tension. But it is also a most valuable piece of social history, bringing to life that significant and exciting period when women struggled to take the right to vote.

First published in 1907, *The Convert* is an insider's view:
'All of it comes from life, Elizabeth Robins' own, Christabel and Emmeline Pankhursts' and the women of all classes who made the suffrage movement work . . . it blurs the borders between art and propaganda, history and fiction . . . It is also a funny, moving and beautifully structured novel'   Jane Marcus

Fiction £2.95

CHARLOTTE PERKINS GILMAN
The Charlotte Perkins Gilman Reader
Introduced and edited by Ann J Lane

This collection brings together the work of a courageous and forward-looking American feminist — much of it for the first time in book form. From the classic 'The Yellow Wallpaper' and other short stories, to excerpts from four novels and three utopias, Charlotte Perkins Gilman brings a playful and incisive mind to bear upon problems which still concern us.

'In her fiction she suggests the kind of world we could have if we worked at it; the kinds of choices we could make, if we insisted on them; the kinds of relationships we could achieve, if we went ahead and demanded them'   Ann J Lane

Fiction   £2.95

CHARLOTTE PERKINS GILMAN
Herland

Three men, turn-of-the-century explorers, set out to find a country of Amazons from which no man has ever returned. Herland is their goal, a country where goodness, strength, intellect, health and beauty are the ideals of all, and where sacred motherhood can be achieved without men.

Herland is a country without class, divisions, war, greed, money, disease, lust or hate. The explorers' embedded notions of 'how things are' turn upside down as all their 'laws' of role playing and gender assignment are daily broken in the life of Herland.

Written in 1915, but not published in book form until 1979, this novel was inspired by the feminist and socialist ideals of its day. Alive with humour and hope, it generates joy and inspiration for us too.

Fiction £1.95